BEST PRACTICES
IN GLOBAL
INVESTOR RELATIONS

BEST PRACTICES IN GLOBAL INVESTOR RELATIONS

The Creation of Shareholder Value

Richard B. Higgins
Foreword by Mark W. Begor

Q

QUORUM BOOKS
Westport, Connecticut • London

Library of Congress Cataloging-in-Publication Data

Higgins, Richard B.
  Best practices in global investor relations : the creation of shareholder value / Richard
  B. Higgins ; foreword by Mark W. Begor.
      p.   cm.
  Includes bibliographical references and index.
  ISBN 1–56720–248–9 (alk. paper)
      1. Corporations—Investor relations.   I. Title.
HD2744.H46   2000
658.4—dc21   99–059846

British Library Cataloguing in Publication Data is available.

Library of Congress Catalog Card Number: 99–059846
ISBN: 1–56720–248–9

First published in 2000

Quorum Books, 88 Post Road West, Westport, CT 06881
An imprint of Greenwood Publishing Group, Inc.
www.quorumbooks.com

Printed in the United States of America

The paper used in this book complies with the
Permanent Paper Standard issued by the National
Information Standards Organization (Z39.48–1984).

10 9 8 7 6 5 4 3

Copyright Acknowledgment

The author and publisher gratefully acknowledge permission for use of the following
material:

Excerpts from NIRI, "Utilizing Technology in the Practice of Investor Relations," used
with permission of the National Investor Relations Institute.

To my wife Sandra, who has been a full partner and vital participant in a project that has been a joint venture from the very beginning.

Her constant encouragement, continuous support, and invaluable contributions have made this book possible.

Contents

Figures and Tables

FIGURES

TABLES

Foreword

Investor relations (IR) has quickly evolved in the 1990s from a reactive communications role to a proactive, high-energy, fast-paced, strategic communications and marketing process. At the same time, investor relations leaders have increasingly shifted from the public-relations and treasury functions to direct daily contact with the CEO and CFO. Today, investor relations is a critical corporate process owned by the CEO.

At General Electric, several factors have contributed to the success of its investor communications program. First and foremost, investor communications is owned by Jack Welch and the GE leadership team. The IR leader at GE is one of 125 GE officers and sits on GE's Corporate Executive Council (CEC). GE's CEC is comprised of Jack Welch's staff and the leaders from each GE business and meets quarterly for two days to review GE's strategy and direction. Involvement by IR at the top of GE ensures a current, clear, and complete message to investors. It is critical that IR is involved in setting the strategy of the business. Second and equally important to GE's IR program is its active involvement directly with investors. Investors—both institutions and individuals—want to put a face and name with a company. GE maintains a constant drumbeat of communications and meetings with investors. GE has an aggressive pace of quarterly meetings in New York, with 200 to 300 investors, monthly lunches and dinners with GE leaders, monthly trips to GE plants and sites around the world, visits to institutions in two to three cities per week across the United States, quarterly meetings in Europe and daily interactions with sell-side and key buy-side analysts, and on and on. This second priority at GE is based on the premise that "face time" with investors is critical and the theory that if GE is not meeting or communicating with investors, another company will be. Our objective is to keep GE at the front of investors' minds. The last priority at GE is to have complete accessibility to its investors. The company treats each investor as it would its very best customer, by being responsive, proactive, accurate, and complete regarding any request or communication. These three factors—a direct connection to top management, an aggressive pace of communications, and complete accessibility to investors—have made GE's IR program successful.

The pace of communications and change in today's global marketplace, along with the thousands of institutions and millions of individuals around the world investing in equities, has become increasingly complex, with thousands and thousands of global investment alternatives. Communicating a clear, concise, and meaningful message to those investors is critical. *Best Practices in Global Investor Relations* provides a broad set of perspectives, lessons learned, and best practices in global investor relations. Dick Higgins examines the fundamentals of investor relations from both a theoretical and a practical level. *Best Practices in Global Investor Relations* includes six case studies from leading global investor relations organizations: AT&T, Schering-Plough, BASF, Reuters, Sony, and Toyota. Each case study reviews individual strategies and challenges for investor relations in unique and meaningful situations.

As the former investor relations leader at GE, I believe *Best Practices in Global Investor Relations* is a must-read for both new and seasoned IR professionals interested in expanding and broadening their perspectives on investor communications. In today's increasingly fast-paced environment, investor relations executives need to continually enhance their investor communications process and search out new ideas to maintain their edge.

Mark W. Begor
Executive Vice President and
Chief Financial Officer, NBC

Acknowledgments

In our earlier book, *The Search for Corporate Strategic Credibility: Concepts and Cases in Global Strategy Communications* (Quorum Books, 1996), the major focus was on the purpose, payoffs, and pitfalls of open strategic and financial communications. We explored questions such as, "Why should companies become actively engaged in investor relations?" and "What are the potential benefits and downside risks?" The primary thrust of this book is, "How to do it," or, more specifically, "How world-class investor relations companies 'do it'—leveraging their strategic and financial communications to gain competitive advantage."

As in our earlier work, we are indebted for the continuing support of the Investor Relations Associations in the United States, France, Germany, the United Kingdom, and Japan. We would like to thank Louis M. Thompson, Jr., president and CEO of the National Investor Relations Institute (NIRI) for NIRI's assistance in administering our 1998 global strategy communications survey. We also wish to express our appreciation to NIRI for their permission to publish the results of their April 1998 study, "Utilizing Technology in the Practice of Investor Relations," conducted by the Rivel Research Group.

Ray DeAngelo, senior vice president of the Association for Investment Management Research (AIMR) continues to be an immense source of support in our ongoing research activities. In the fall of 1998 AIMR and Stratcom Associates collaborated in the design and administration of a questionnaire survey of AIMR's membership. The pur-

xiv   Acknowledgments

pose of the study was to explore the use of new technologies such as the Internet and e-mail by companies followed by AIMR members (primarily analysts and portfolio managers).

We would like to thank Harold Haddock, Jr., former chief financial officer, Price-Waterhouse, and Tony Parra, former investor relations officer, NYNEX, for their many helpful comments and suggestions during the design of the AIMR technology survey questionnaire. Also, our appreciation to Benn Boulton, president, Computer Comfort, Inc., who did an outstanding job in the programming, data tabulation and analysis, and graphic display of questionnaire survey results. The NIRI and AIMR technology survey results are reported in Chapter 5.

In addition, we would like to thank Kate Hoyle of the British Investor Relations Society for her support and assistance in administering the 1998 global strategy communications survey to a sample of society members. Klaus D. Jessen, investor relations manager at BASF, again, as in our earlier book, continues to wear two hats: Representing the German Investor Relations Association (DIRK), Klaus assisted us with the 1998 communications survey update. As a contributing author, he updated the BASF case, which first appeared in *The Search for Corporate Strategic Credibility*. Yoshiko Sato performed similar yeoman service. As program director and senior research fellow of the Japan Investor Relations Association (JIRA), she continues to support our research activities, administering the 1998 global strategy communications survey to a sample of the JIRA membership. She is also a major contributing author to our latest book, authoring two chapters. Also, we would like to thank Francois Archambault, investor relations director at L'Oreal, for his assistance in administering our 1998 communications update survey to members of the French Investor Relations Society (CLIFF).

We are deeply indebted to Constantine Spiliotes, professor at Dartmouth College, and his student, Louisa Serene, for their invaluable assistance in the programming, tabulation, and analysis of the 1998 global strategy communication survey data. The results of this survey are reported in Chapter 4.

At this point we must acknowledge a huge debt of gratitude to the principal architects of this book—those individuals who have taken time from their busy schedules and demanding duties to record and reflect upon the best practices in global investor relations that the companies reported in this book: Mark W. Begor, executive vice president and chief financial officer, NBC, who contributed the Foreword; Geraldine U. Foster, senior vice president, investor relations and corporate communications, and Stephen K. Galpin, Jr., staff vice president, corporate communications, both of Schering-Plough Corporation, coauthors of Chapter 7; Peter Gregson, corporate publications manager, Reuters PLC, coauthor of Chapter 9; Klaus D. Jessen, investor relations manager, BASF, author of Chapter 8; Yoshiko Sato, program director and senior research fellow, Japan Investor Relations Association (JIRA), author of Chapter 10 and coauthor of Chapter 11; Connie Weaver, vice president, investor relations and communications at AT&T, author of Chapter 6; Geoffrey Wicks, director, corporate relations, Reuters PLC, coauthor of Chapter 9; and Toru Yoshikawa, lecturer at the College of Commerce, Nihon University, Tokyo, coauthor of Chapter 11. Also, special thanks to Frederick K. Malley and Guido Schlesinger of AT&T, Paula Hagen of Schering-Plough, and Mary Lowengard, consultant and editor of *Investor Relations Quarterly*, for their many contributions to the book.

To all the authors and contributors to this book, it has been my pleasure and privilege to have had the opportunity to work with each and every one of you. It has been a rich and rewarding experience for me. Thank you, one and all.

Finally, a word of appreciation to Eric Valentine, publisher of Quorum Books. In late fall 1997 I made a proposal to Eric to revise our earlier work, *The Search for Corporate Strategic Credibility*. It was to be a modest revision, perhaps adding two or three new company cases, an update of our 1993 global strategy communications survey, and a review of recent research in the field of strategic and financial communications. On more than one occasion since then, I have wondered what ever happened to that modest revision. How did we get from there to here? Was it the "pull" of doing another book in a field that I have become increasingly fascinated with (global investor relations)? Or was it a "push" by our esteemed publisher? Push or pull, I continue to enjoy working with my friend, Eric Valentine. I would not have undertaken this project with any other publisher.

No listing of acknowledgments would be complete without expressing my deep appreciation to Sandra D. Higgins and Libbett Watson, who performed magnificently, translating my barely legible scribblings into something that can be read—and, hopefully, enjoyed.

1

Introduction

This is a book about the "best practices" of six companies with outstanding investor relations (IR) programs. We will examine the strategic communications activities of each of these leading, global corporations as they interact with the investment community. The major purpose of the book is to extract and distill lessons to be learned from the successful practice of corporate strategic and financial communications.

However, the book is intended to be more than a collection of selected company case studies. Impinging upon the communications practices of virtually all global corporations are a number of institutional, market, and technological forces that are shaping the current practice of investor relations. We will examine these forces and their impact on strategic and financial communications. We will also explore the theoretical and empirical foundations underpinning the practice of investor relations and present a conceptual model, a strategic perspective, for viewing and analyzing the "best practices" of our six leading strategic and financial communications companies.

In our earlier book, *The Search for Corporate Strategic Credibility: Concepts and Cases in Global Strategy Communications*, published in 1996, the focus was on the risks and rewards of engaging in candid, specific, and timely strategic communications with the investment community.[1] We explored the payoffs and pitfalls associated with the conduct of open communications, as well as the consequences of "strategic stonewalling," that is, failing to engage in candid communications behavior (in the absence of sound strategic and financial information, analysts and others tend to assume the worst).

The focus of this book shifts from the question, "Why do it?" (engage in active investor relations), to the question, "How to do it?" or, more precisely, "How do leading corporate strategic and financial communications companies do it?" We will look at how investor relations are practiced at several world-premier strategic and financial communications companies. The following questions drive the basic inquiry of this book:

1. Why are these companies so highly regarded within the investment community? How have they earned their reputations for excellence in corporate strategic and financial communications?

2. Do they do the same things that other companies do, the everyday, routine things, practicing the basic, time-tested principles of sound communications, but doing so more effectively than other companies?

3. Do these leading companies do different things—unique, creative, innovative things—that set them apart from others in their industries? How have they managed to become pioneers, leading the way for the rest of the field?

4. In short, what makes these companies outstanding in their strategic and financial communications and investor relations?

OVERVIEW OF THIS BOOK

Part I (Chapters 2–5) presents the conceptual, empirical, technological, and institutional foundations of corporate strategic and financial communications. In Chapter 2, we provide a conceptual framework, a model of "strategic credibility," to establish a theoretical context and strategic perspective for viewing and analyzing the strategic and financial communications practices reported in Part II of the book. In presenting this model, the General Electric Company (GE) is offered as a classic example of a corporation that enjoys high levels of strategic credibility. The results of an empirical test of our strategic credibility model are also included in this chapter, as well as research findings and anecdotal evidence associated with the determinants of strategic credibility.

In Chapter 3 we will examine the current state of corporate strategic and financial communications and investors relations, in terms of theory, research, and current practice. In the inaugural issue of *Investor Relations Quarterly*, the basic question, "Why Investor Relations?" was raised prominently on the front cover. The journal offered some compelling answers to the question, in terms of research findings that point to the positive payoffs derived from active investor relations, as well as the economic, legal, and institutional forces that have combined to encourage more open strategic and financial communications practices.[2] We will explore these payoffs in Chapter 3.

In Chapter 4, we will look at some of the challenges of global strategy communications, revisiting a 1993 international survey that was reported in *The Search for Corporate Strategic Credibility*.[3] In 1993, 1,866 investor relations officers and security analysts in the United States, the United Kingdom, France, Germany, and Japan were surveyed by means of a questionnaire that asked respondents to evaluate and comment on the investor relations practices in their own companies and countries. An analysis of cross-cultural differences among countries, as well as institutional differences (investor relations officers versus security analysts), revealed some interesting, if perhaps not surprising, results.

In Chapter 4, we report on the results of a five-year update of our earlier "1993 Global Strategy Communications Survey." This time, 790 investor relations officers in the United States, the United Kingdom, France, Germany, and Japan were surveyed. Because of the low response rate of security analysts in the 1993 survey, we did not include analysts in the 1998 update.

We were interested in discovering if there had been any discernible changes in IR practices and attitudes in the past five years. Given the increased globalization of capital markets in the intervening years, we were particularly interested in testing two hypotheses:

Hypothesis #1—As the globalization of capital markets proceeds, country and regional differences in IR practices and attitudes toward corporate strategic and financial communications will tend to diminish. This trend toward convergence in worldwide communications attitudes and practices will continue as capital markets continue to globalize.

Hypothesis #2—Overall, the level of openness in corporate strategic and financial communications will increase, as institutional and market forces compel more open disclosure. These forces will countervail the influence of cultural forces that tend to discourage more open communications.

Results of the 1998 survey were used to test these hypotheses and are featured in Chapter 4.

Chapter 5 examines the technological revolution that is impacting the current practice of investor relations. As the use of conference calls, the Internet, e-mail, and fax machines has expanded in just the past year or two, the possibility of instant access to large quantities of detailed, current, strategic, and financial information is becoming a reality for investors, analysts, and government regulators (the Security and Exchange Commission [SEC], for one). "Transparency" is sweeping into capital markets even as they are globalizing.

In Chapter 5, we report on the results of two recent surveys:

1. *Utilizing Technology in the Practice of Investor Relations*—This ongoing study of Senior Investor Relations Executives at NIRI companies (members of the National Investor Relations Institute) seeks to determine current practices in the use of new technologies in investor relations activities.

2. *Using Technology and the Internet: Researching Corporate Strategic and Financial Information*—This is a study conducted by the Association for Investment Management and Research (AIMR) to examine the use that security analysts are making of new technologies in following their companies. Also, the survey seeks to evaluate the quality of corporate strategic and financial information that companies are providing the investment community by means of these new technologies.

In Part II of the book (Chapters 6–11) we will examine the corporate strategic and financial practices of six leading global communications and investor relations companies. Chapter 6 looks at the investor communications practices at AT&T during a period of technological revolution in the U.S. communications industry. Emerging technology is fast eliminating the barriers that now separate local, long distance, Internet, entertainment, and wireless services. As AT&T seeks to become a lead contestant in what it calls the "any distance" marketplace, the role of investor communications becomes critical in articulating and gaining support among shareholders for AT&T's bold new strategic vision. In particular, this chapter takes a close look at the operation of a newly constructed IR Web site at AT&T. Using the Internet as a strategic tool, the company has been largely successful in keeping shareholders abreast of management actions (acquisitions and joint ventures) taken to achieve a leadership position in this new and revolutionary marketplace.

Chapter 7 examines the investor relations practices at Schering-Plough Corporation (SGP), the highly successful U.S. pharmaceutical and health-care company. Schering-Plough has received the number-one Award for Excellence in Corporate Reporting from AIMR for an unprecedented six consecutive years. Included in this chapter is a discussion of the philosophy, strategy, and structure of Schering-Plough's unique investor relations program. Also in the chapter is a description of a number of pioneering IR practices that have received commendation by AIMR—innovative and creative disclosure practices and IR publications—and have been well received by analysts and portfolio managers and emulated by other health-care companies.[4]

Chapter 8, which is an updated and expanded version of a chapter that first appeared in *The Search for Corporate Strategic Credibility*, examines the strategic role of corporate financial communications and investor relations at BASF, the diversified German chemical manufacturer.[5] As an early pioneer in investor relations in Germany, BASF's corporate financial communications program has won a number of prestigious industry awards. What persuaded the company of the need to establish an investor relations function and why did BASF feel the need to do so before other German companies? How are the functions of corporate financial communications and investor relations organized and integrated with other functions, such as public relations, legal, accounting, and strategic planning? What accounts for the willingness of top-management team members at BASF to be actively involved in investor relations, given a tradition and culture in many German companies that discourage such activities? These and other questions are explored in Chapter 8, along with an update of IR activities at BASF, including several innovative financial communications practices recently developed.

Reuters PLC, the subject of Chapter 9, has built a global business supplying information electronically, and the related products and services used to deliver, manage, manipulate, and deal with information. It is a wholesaler to the global financial community. In 1997 Reuters was ranked as Britain's Most Admired Company in a survey conducted by *Management Today*.[6] Chapter 9 explores the investor relations program at Reuters. One reason why Reuters needs to run an effective and transparent IR program is that their major investors are also their clients. Not only does Reuters rely on sound IR communications practices and principles—that is, "communicate with the financial community in bad times as well as good"—they have also pioneered in a number of innovative technology applications in their IR activities. These are also discussed in Chapter 9.

Chapter 10 takes a look at the corporate strategic and financial communications practices at the global electronics giant, the Sony Corporation. A recipient of several awards for disclosure, both in Japan and in other countries, Sony also was ranked number one among Japanese companies in our 1998 Global Strategy Communications Survey.[7] Since Sony was listed on the New York Stock Exchange (NYSE), their investor relations activities have received support and commitment from top management, resulting in an active, consistent, and effective IR program. Chapter 10 examines how Sony has managed to reconcile an activist approach to investor relations with traditional Japanese management practices.

Chapter 11 explores the corporate strategic and financial communications practices of the Japanese automaker, Toyota, another company that has been successful in penetrating global markets while retaining a management style rooted in the Japanese culture. Toyota was ranked number two among Japanese companies in our 1998 Survey of Global Strategy Communications.[8] This chapter also looks at the difficult times facing the Japanese automobile industry and how Toyota is responding to these challenges. The impact of these challenges, including a distressed Asian economy, on the practice of investor relations at Toyota is examined. Toyota's IR program is also compared with the financial communications of its major Japanese competitors, Nissan and Honda.

In Part III of the book, Chapter 12 presents the lessons to be learned from the corporate strategic and financial communications practices at six leading global communications companies. Effectiveness in investor relations at these companies has been achieved through a combination of factors, including the following:

- A creative synthesis of innovative IR activities and practices grounded in sound communications principles, leveraged by the latest applications of new technologies.
- The commitment and active involvement of senior management.
- A seamless communications web achieved through an integrated and coordinated effort among senior management, corporate communications, and investor relations professionals.
- A persistent pursuit of candid and open corporate strategic and financial communications in bad times and good.

A synergistic interaction of all of these factors has propelled these companies' communications programs to the world-class level.

NOTES

1. Richard B. Higgins, *The Search for Corporate Strategic Credibility: Concepts and Cases in Global Strategy Communications* (Westport, Conn.: Quorum Books, 1996).

2. *Investor Relations Quarterly* 1, no. 1 (1997): entire inaugural issue.

3. Higgins, *Search for Corporate Strategic Credibility*, 131–146.

4. Corporate Information Committee, Association for Investment Management and Research, "1995–96 Annual Review of Corporate Reporting Practices," 28.

5. Higgins, *Search for Corporate Strategic Credibility*, 109–127.

6. "Britain's Most Admired Companies, 1997," *Management Today*, December 1997.

7. Higgins, *Search for Corporate Strategic Credibility*, 145.

8. Ibid.

—————————————————————— PART I

CONCEPTUAL, INSTITUTIONAL, AND TECHNOLOGICAL FOUNDATIONS

2

Strategic Credibility

You can't grow long-term if you can't eat short-term. . . . Anybody can manage short. Anybody can manage long. Balancing those two things is what management is.[1]

John F. Welch, Jr.,
Chairman and Chief Executive Officer,
General Electric Company

As a corporate pioneer in the development of strategic planning systems and with a long procession of highly regarded top managements, the General Electric Company (GE) has been largely successful over the years in communicating the message that their success is planned—not accidental.[2] For several decades the company has enjoyed high levels of strategic credibility. However, in its 1988 annual report GE referred to two major disappointments. One was a quality problem with its new refrigerator compressors, leading to a costly replacement program. The other was a share price that did not appear to keep pace with the firm's recent strong performance. Earnings per share rose 17 percent in both 1987 and 1988; return on shareholders equity increased from 17.7 percent in 1986 to 18.5 percent in 1987 and to 19.4 percent in 1988. In addition, the company's balance sheet and cash flow remained strong during this period.

The fact that the firm's share price failed to reflect this strong performance was due, in large part, to a perception by outsiders that GE's strategy was not focused—or so the company suggested: "Especially in 1988, we began hearing: GE is 'too difficult to understand' and 'portfolio managing.' We even heard ourselves described by the 'C' word—conglomerate—and with its usual pejorative corollary: 'Who knows what they'll buy or sell next?'"[3]

The company acknowledged, "Those who track us in the financial analysts community or financial press have more homework to do than those who watch and report on our peers. We have businesses ranging from plastics to network broadcasting to the manufacture of jet engines to reinsurance. But the strategy, the management philosophy that drives the company, is the essence of simplicity."[4]

Nonetheless, the company accepted partial responsibility for what they believed were inaccurate perceptions held by outsiders: "Perhaps a strategy that appears to us crystal clear and consistent—because we live by it—seems less so to some of our constituencies in the media and financial community. This is more likely a failure of our communication efforts."[5] The remainder of the letter to shareholders in the 1988 annual report was devoted to a detailed explanation of GE's corporate strategy.

It is ironic that GE found itself in this position. The company and its chairman and CEO Jack Welch have been quite open about their strategy over the years. GE has been cited on several occasions for their excellence in corporate communications by the Financial Analysts Federation (now the Association for Investment Management and Research). Prior to the stock market crash in 1987, the company enjoyed a solid price–earnings multiple; after that, its multiple declined. The problem did not seem to be with results or performance directly. Nor did it appear to be a function of ineffective communications or a lack of top management (CEO) credibility. The issue seemed to be more a question of the perceived soundness of GE's corporate strategy. Did their acquisitions and divestments make sense? While the RCA acquisition received high marks from most, there can be little doubt that the company stumbled with the Kidder Peabody acquisition. Wondering whether GE had embarked on a conglomerate strategy, one security analyst observed, "GE, in my opinion, does not have a clear picture of itself. It has an acquisition strategy that has not been rationalized."[6]

Fast forward ten years. This is what analysts and GE observers were saying in 1998:

"The two greatest corporate leaders of this century are Alfred Sloan of General Motors and Jack Welch of GE," says Noel Tichy, a longtime GE observer and University of Michigan management professor. "And Welch would be the greater of the two because he set a new contemporary paradigm for the corporation that is the model for the 21st century."

It is a model that has delivered extraordinary growth, increasing the market value of GE from just $12 billion in 1981 [the year that Welch became CEO and chairman], to about $280 billion today. No one, not Microsoft's William H. Gates III or Intel's Andrew S. Grove, not Walt Disney's Michael D. Eisner or Berkshire Hathaway's Warren E. Buffett, not even the late Coca-Cola chieftain Roberto C. Goizueta or the late Wal-Mart founder Sam Walton has created more shareholder value than Jack Welch. So giddy are some Wall Street analysts at GE's prospects that they believe that when Welch leaves at the end of 2000, GE's stock could trade at $150 to $200 a share, up from $82 now and the company could be worth $490 billion to $650 billion.[7]

STRATEGIC CREDIBILITY

Without a doubt, the General Electric Company and John F. Welch Jr. enjoy enormous amounts of strategic credibility. Just what is "strategic credibility" and what are the major determinants of strategic credibility? How are some companies, like GE, able to sustain high levels of strategic credibility over time, while other companies either watch their credibility ebb and flow or never manage to achieve it?

Strategic credibility is in the eyes of the beholders, key stakeholders and corporate constituencies who define a company's credibility according to their understanding of its performance, goals, and strategic soundness. Does the strategic thrust of the firm make sense? Is it reliable and believable? Strategic credibility, as defined in this book, is more specific that the general notion of corporate image. It is also more focused than the concept of corporate reputation developed by *Fortune* magazine, although there is probably some overlap—most notably under two attributes of reputation used by *Fortune*—"quality of management" and "financial soundness."

"Strategic credibility must be earned, not fabricated out of glib phrases from communications specialists."[8] "The good news is that strategic credibility can be managed."[9] What are the major determinants of strategic credibility? What are the potential payoffs associated with a positive strategic reputation? The author and associates have been engaged in an ongoing study searching for answers to these questions. Security analysts and corporate executives have been surveyed; corporate communications documents, such as annual reports, have been examined; transcripts of CEO speeches to security analysts have been reviewed; literature dealing with corporate image, reputation, and credibility has been explored. This chapter provides a conceptual framework—a model of strategic credibility, its determinants, associated payoffs, and potential benefits. Also included are the results of an empirical test of the model: a survey of 419 U.S. security analysts drawn from the membership directory of the Financial Analysts Federation.

DETERMINANTS OF STRATEGIC CREDIBILITY

Strategic credibility is determined by an interplay of a number of factors. Chief among them are (1) a company's strategic capability, (2) past corporate performance, (3) the credibility of the firm's top management team, most notably the chief executive officer, and (4) communication of corporate strategy to key stakeholders (see Figure 2.1).

STRATEGIC CAPABILITY

A major component of a company's strategic credibility is based on its perceived strategic capability. In turn, a firm's strategic capability is determined by the soundness of its corporate strategy and the effectiveness of its strategic planning process. The strategy must embody a strategic view of the future and a plan designed to achieve strategic goals and objectives. The strategic vision must be responsive to emerging opportunities and sensitive to the internal strengths of the company. As the multinational corporation gives way to the transnational organization, the soundness of a firm's global strategy will also be

Figure 2.1
Strategic Credibility Model

Source: Reprinted from *Long Range Planning,* 25, Richard B. Higgins and Brendan D. Bannister, "How Corporate Communication of Strategy Affects Share Price," p. 28, Copyright 1992, with permission from Elsevier Science.

measured by how well it meets two sometimes conflicting demands: the need to achieve global economies of scale and to respond to differences in various geographical markets.

Strategic planning effectiveness is based on an adaptive, successive planning process that continually scans the behavior of key competitors. The structure of the planning process must integrate a company's operational and financial plans with strategic plans and overall corporate objectives so that, in the words of one security analyst, "It all melds together."[10] Such an integrated, adaptive planning process increases the likelihood of a continuing future stream of sound strategic decisions.

Ten years after some analysts seriously questioned the very essence of GE's corporate strategy, the strategic capability of the General Electric Company dominates the global corporate landscape. Based on its renowned strategic planning capability as well as the now-acknowledged soundness of its global corporate strategy, GE indeed appears to have created "a new contemporary paradigm for the corporation . . . a model for the 21st century."[11]

PAST CORPORATE PERFORMANCE

Studies that have examined the relationship between strategic planning and corporate performance have led to mixed results. Welch and Rhyne reported a significant, positive relationship between planning and performance.[12] Frederickson and Mitchell and Leontiades and Tezel found no such connection.[13] Our model views this relationship as more complex. Both a firm's strategic capability and superior corporate performance contribute to strategic credibility. However, the absence of one does not necessarily result in a major loss of credibility, at least in the short run. One can imagine a firm lacking a sustainable strategic capability but enjoying strong performance, due primarily to being in the right industry at the right time. People Express in the early years of airline deregulation is a case in point. On the other hand, a firm battling a prolonged industry slump may experience a temporary downturn in performance without suffering an immediate erosion of credibility. While the investment community becomes restive in the face of sustained poor performance, in the short run the company with highly regarded strategic capabilities but showing soft performance may continue to retain a measure of strategic credibility. DuPont in chemicals and Chrysler in the automobile industry were examples in the mid-1990s. What may be most important here is how candid and effective the firm is in discussing their problems and what they intend to do about them. Of course, ultimately, strategic capability must be translated into superior corporate performance if credibility is to be maintained. IBM learned this painful lesson the hard way in the early 1990s.

On the other hand, the corporate performance of GE for the past eighteen years, with Welch leading General Electric to one revenue and earnings record after another, has been a major ingredient in the company's sustained, high levels of strategic credibility.

CEO CREDIBILITY

A company's strategic credibility is also enhanced by the reputation and image projected by its chief executive officer. If the CEO is highly visible, widely known and respected, and effective in communicating the company's future direction, the firm's strategic reputation may be bolstered. In *Fortune's* global survey, "The Most Admired Companies in the World," GE's number-one ranking in their industry undoubtedly is at least partially attributable to the strategic stature of Jack Welch.[14] Other examples of "credibility transference" abound. Hubie Clark at Baker International, Edward Hennessey at Allied Signal, and Donald Melville at the Norton Company all were successful in projecting their own image in a way that enhanced their company's strategic credibility. Can a CEO's strategic stature be transplanted from one company to another? Apparently Eastman Kodak thought so when they brought in George Fisher from Motorola. While the move did little to diminish Motorola's reputation (they retained their number-one industry ranking by *Fortune* in 1995), Kodak jumped three places in their industry ranking under the new CEO. (It is much less clear whether the intangible, personal qualities frequently associated with CEO credibility can be passed along to successor CEOs.) Finally, it should be noted that the reverse also holds true. If the CEO does not project a strong strategic image, it may be difficult to convince anyone that the company has a sound strategy and planning process.

CORPORATE STRATEGY COMMUNICATIONS

A final determinant in our strategic credibility model is communication of corporate strategy to key stakeholders. The Financial Analysts Federation observed,

Credibility is an intangible, but analysts often find that the market place can better accept a company's securities if it senses the presence of corporate direction and responsibility. Management as well as analysts obviously benefit from the effort to provide investors with clear explanations of corporate goals, objectives and strategies. Better understanding of company performance and objectives on the part of others who read financial reports—employees and customers, chief among them—is a further logical reason for substantive and focused corporate reporting.[15]

Drawn from the literature on communications and message character-istics are three items that appear to be particularly important: communi-cations openness, communications specificity, and communications timeliness.[16] How open is a company in the disclosure of important strategic information? How specific is the information provided to key stakeholders? When situations arise that require the prompt disclo-sure of strategic information, how timely are the company's strategic communications? Another significant communication characteristic is found in the literature dealing with self-serving attributions. How can-did is the company in discussing its performance accomplishments and disappointments? Do they claim major credit for their successes, while blaming failures on uncontrollable, external factors?

Peter Anastas, financial analyst and vice president of New York–based Alliance Capital Management, discusses these and other char-acteristics as he outlines the criteria he uses when evaluating a firm's corporate communications program:

Consistency: When I look at a series of annual reports, I like to see some consis-tency in style, in culture and in the way management strategizes. And, of course, I like to see some consistency between what they said they were going to do and what they've done.

Credibility: I like to see some credibility or candidness about how operations are really going. I want a straight-forwardness of style—a minimum of hype and a maximum of information.

Clarity: You can be credible, but not necessarily clear in what you're saying. You can be obtuse. Or you can be so involved in the specifics of your busi-ness that you don't share with me something more important, the grand scheme (i.e., strategy) of things—What's really going on now and what will be happening over the next several years.[17]

Credibility and candor are frequently strained in the management of "good news" and "bad news." The story of the Colgate-Palmolive annual report for 1984, as discussed in *New York* magazine, is a case in point: The company's earnings had dipped to $0.86 per share from the previous year's $2.42 per share, with a loss of $1.13 in the fourth quar-ter alone. "Working capital had fallen to its lowest level in five years. Total assets were below those of 1982. And shareholder equity and book value had dropped to the lowest levels since 1979."[18] How were shareholders informed of this disquieting news? The annual report's letter to shareholders began in big, bold type, "Colgate-Palmolive to-day sells over 3,000 products in 135 countries." It took six paragraphs (and countless glowing comments) before Colgate finally disclosed those disastrous 1984 earnings numbers—the typeface used for their dismal profit showing was much lighter and smaller. One paragraph later, the message returned to boldface.[19]

On the other hand, the General Electric Company has long been recognized for its openness in communicating with the investment community. As mentioned earlier, they have been cited on several occasions for their "Excellence in Corporate Communications." In the Association for Investment Management and Research's *1995–96 Annual Review of Corporate Reporting Practices*, the Electrical Equipment Committee of AIMR offered the following assessment of GE's corporate reporting practices:

The investor program of . . . General Electric is excellent. The company's annual report is essential reading for analysts and investor relations professionals. The Chairman's Letter clearly states the company's strategy, decision-making process and direction. General Electric's investor relations professionals are accessible and responsive. The company has arranged frequent information meetings on specific business units and recently has begun to hold meetings to discuss how themes such as globalization and service are being implemented in G.E. operating businesses. Presentations at least twice a year by the chairman offered significant insight into company and industry issues as well as investor concerns.[20]

STRATEGIC CREDIBILITY MODEL: SUMMARY COMMENTS

The high level of strategic credibility that the General Electric Company has enjoyed over many years is hard earned. The company has consistently demonstrated a superior strategic capability. Its strategic and financial performance year in and year out is the envy of its competitors and the delight of its shareholders, who have reaped the greatest increase in shareholder value in American business history. The credibility of its CEO and chairman is legendary and, some say, destined to land him in business and economic history books as one of the two most influential business executives of the twentieth century. The General Electric Company's award-winning corporate strategic and financial communications program is well documented. Small wonder, then, that GE's strategic credibility places it consistently among the most admired corporations in the United States and in the world. With powerful anecdotal evidence that strongly suggests that strategic credibility, indeed, does count, the next logical task is to conduct an empirical test of our strategic credibility model.

EMPIRICAL TEST OF STRATEGIC CREDIBILITY MODEL

An empirical test of our strategic credibility model was performed with questionnaires mailed to a random sample of 419 U.S. security analysts drawn from the membership directory of the Financial Analysts Federation. The questionnaire asked each analyst to select and evaluate a company of their choice. This self-selection process was adopted after problems had been encountered in an earlier security-analyst survey in which we had arbitrarily assigned companies to be evaluated by analysts. A substantial number of questionnaires were returned unanswered by analysts, along with the typical comment, "I do not know this company well enough to make an informed evaluation."

Identification of the company was optional. Actually, over two-thirds of all respondents did identify their selected company (which allowed us to relate respondent ratings of company strategic credibility to share price in the case of forty-eight different firms). Analysts were asked to rate their company's strategic capability, its past performance, the credibility of its chief executive officer, its corporate communications practices, and the firm's overall strategic credibility. The overall response rate for the survey was 24.6 percent.

RESULTS: STRATEGIC CREDIBILITY PAYS OFF

Firms varied considerably in their strategic credibility ratings, from a low of 1.88 to a high of 5.0 (on a 5-point Likert scale). Analysts' ratings of strategic capability, corporate performance, CEO credibility, and corporate communications were moderately positive, with all mean scores above the midpoint on the 5-point scale. Analysts' responses also indicated that they did not believe that their companies were self-serving in their attributions of corporate performance (see Table 2.1).[21]

In a statistical analysis of our model, strategic capability emerged as the most influential determinant of strategic credibility; overall corporate communications was identified as the second most significant determinant. (Strategic capability accounted for 67 percent of the variation in strategic credibility among companies. Corporate communications accounted for an additional 9 percent of variation.) Looking at the relationship between more specific communication characteristics and strategic credibility, "openness," "specificity," and "timeliness" of communications all showed strong correlations with strategic credibility. "Communications about the future" also appeared to be a significant characteristic.[22]

To explore the relationship between strategic credibility and share price, we examined a subset of companies included in our survey—

Table 2.1
Mean Values, High and Low Ratings for Major Variables

VARIABLES	LOW	HIGH	MEAN
• Strategic Capability	1.40	5.00	3.63
• Corporate Performance	1.25	5.00	3.71
• CEO Credibility	1.00	5.00	3.88
• Corporate Communications	1.00	5.00	3.53
• Attributions About Performance	1.00	4.50	2.53
• Strategic Credibility	1.88	5.00	3.88
Number of Respondents - 104			

Source: Reprinted from *Long Range Planning*, 25, Richard B. Higgins and Brendan D.
Bannister, "How Corporate Communication of Strategy Affects Share Price," p. 31,
Copyright 1992, with permission from Elsevier Science.

those firms that had been identified by security analysts in their returned questionnaires. These companies (usable returns provided a
sample of forty-eight companies from thirty-four different industries) were
divided into two groups—high-credibility companies and low-credibility firms. Market price/book value (M/B) ratios were then obtained from
Standard and Poor's Compustat Services, Inc.[23] Company M/B ratios were
compared with specific industry average M/B ratios for the years 1985,
1986, and 1987. As Table 2.2 indicates, high strategic credibility companies showed higher M/B values relative to their specific industry
averages than lower strategic credibility firms for all three years. Differences were statistically significant in 1986 and 1987.[24]

CONCLUSION

Twenty-five years after the concept of "strategic management" has
become commonplace in corporate corridors and business school class-
rooms throughout the United States, work remains to be done. Unfortunately, while many managers think strategically, fewer successfully

Table 2.2
Company M/B Ratios Divided by Industry Average M/B Ratio

	1985	1986 [1]	1987 [2]
High Credibility Companies	1.043	1.102	1.177
Low Credibility Companies	.993	.934	.967

Source: Reprinted from *Long Range Planning*, 25, Richard B. Higgins and Brendan D. Bannister, "How Corporate Communication of Strategy Affects Share Price," p. 33, Copyright 1992, with permission from Elsevier Science.
[1]Difference in M/B means, high-credibility companies versus low-credibility companies, statistically significant at the 0.07 level.
[2]Difference in M/B means significant at the 0.05 level.

implement their strategic visions, and fewer still think strategically, act strategically, and communicate strategically. Jack Welch of GE clearly is a champion of all three. By all counts, Welch is a consummate corporate communicator:

Most great leaders, of course, are masters at communicating their desires. In his early years as chief executive, Welch discovered that you can't will things to happen, nor can you simply communicate with a few hundred people at the top and expect change to occur. So he doggedly repeats the key messages over and over again, reinforcing them at every opportunity.... As Thomas E. Dunham, who runs services in G.E. Medical Systems, puts it, "Welch preaches from the top and people see it at the bottom." The result: Welch's leadership style is continually reinforced up and down the organization.[25]

As noted earlier, Welch also appears to be equally adept in communicating with external constituencies.

However, the CEO and chairman of General Electric is probably the exception rather than the rule. Security analysts claim that the strategic information provided by most companies is not very good. When asked about the quality of strategic information made available by the companies that they regularly follow, two-thirds of the analysts described the information as "bland generalities of little use."[26]

Why is this so? Some managers may fear a competitive response to the disclosure of strategic information. Others may feel that strategic communications are not necessary, assuming (frequently wrongly) that key stakeholders already are familiar with the strategic vision and future direction of their company. Other executives may be wary of creating inflated expectations as the result of strategic disclosures. For whatever reason, many companies are forgoing the rewards that might be achieved through open and frank strategic communications.

In Chapter 3, we will explore some of the benefits associated with strategic communications and an activist investor relations approach. We will also examine a number of forces—institutional, global, and technological—that are shaping the current practice of investor relations and tending to open up the process of strategic communications.

NOTES

1. *Business Week*, 8 June 1998, 92.

2. Much of this chapter draws upon expanded and updated material that first appeared in Richard B. Higgins, *The Search for Corporate Strategic Credibility: Concepts and Cases in Global Strategy Communications* (Westport, Conn.: Quorum Books, 1996), 15–33.

3. General Electric Co., *1988 Annual Report*, 1.

4. Ibid.

5. Ibid.

6. *The Wall Street Transcript*, 25 April 1988, 89189.

7. *Business Week*, 8 June 1998, 93.

8. Richard B. Higgins and Brendan D. Bannister, "Corporate Communications: 'Frontrunners' vs. 'Challengers,'" In *1989/1990 Handbook of Business Strategy*, ed. Harold E. Glass (Boston: Warren, Gorham and Lamont, 1990), 1–3.

9. Richard B. Higgins and Brendan D. Bannister, "How Corporate Communication of Strategy Affects Share Price," *Long Range Planning* 25 (June 1992): 27–35.

10. Richard B. Higgins and John Diffenbach, "The Impact of Strategic Planning on Stock Prices," *Journal of Business Strategy* 6 (Fall 1985): 65.

11. *Business Week*, 8 June 1998, 93.

12. J. B. Welch, "Strategic Planning Could Improve Your Share Price," *Long Range Planning* 17, no. 2 (1984): 144–147; Lawrence C. Rhyne, "The Relationship of Strategic Planning to Financial Performance," *Strategic Management Journal* 7 (1986): 423–436.

13. J. W. Frederickson and T. R. Mitchell, "Strategic Decision Processes: Comprehensiveness and Performance in an Industry with an Unstable Environment," *Academy of Management Journal* 27 (1984): 399–423; M. Leontiades and A. Tezel, "Planning Perception and Planning Results," *Strategic Management Journal* 1 (1980): 65–76.

14. *Fortune*, 27 October 1997, 220.

15. Financial Analysts Federation, *1985–1986 Corporate Information Committee Report*, 8.

16. D. Ilgen, C. Fisher, and M. S. Taylor, "Consequences of Individual Feedback on Behavior in Organizations," *Journal of Applied Psychology* 64 (1979): 349–371.

17. From interview with Peter Anastas published in Rose DeNeve, *Annual Report Trends*, no. 4 (Boston: S. D. Warren Idea Exchange Library of Printed Samples, 1987), 37–38.

18. Dan Dorfman, "The Bottom Line: The Worst Annual Reports," *New York*, 10 June 1985, 17.

19. Ibid.

20. Association for Investment Management and Research, *1995–1996 Annual Review of Corporate Reporting Practices*, 17.

21. Higgins and Bannister, "How Corporate Communication of Strategy Affects Share Price," 31.

22. Brendan D. Bannister and Richard B. Higgins, "Strategic Capability, Corporate Communications and Strategic Credibility," *Journal of Managerial Issues* 5 (Spring 1993): 99.

23. Compustat II, 16 February 1989.

24. Higgins and Bannister, "How Corporate Communication of Strategy Affects Share Price," 30.

25. *Business Week*, 8 June 1998, 99, 102.

26. Higgins and Diffenbach, "Impact of Strategic Planning on Stock Prices," 67.

3

Current State of Investor Relations: Theory and Practice

The National Investor Relations Institute defines investors' relations as a strategic corporate marketing activity, combining the disciplines of communication and finance, providing present and potential investors with an accurate portrayal of a company's performance and prospects.[1]

Louis M. Thompson, Jr., President and CEO,
National Investor Relations Institute

Today, investor relations is not only a job that entails communicating a company's strategic direction, it is a discipline that requires its own strategic design. Borrowing from techniques practiced by marketing professionals, investor relations has evolved from a passive practice to an active one, where investors are truly regarded as "customers" owning the company's equity. In just ten short years, investor relations has not only come of age, it has come into its own as a profession in its own right. . . . Further, the practice of investor relations is no longer confined to the individual titled as "director" or "manager." Every time the senior management of a company speaks to any audience, they are practicing investor relations. In today's technologically advanced society, all words get through to investors and other related parties. Every press release issued, no matter how trivial, is part of investor relations. . . . The degree to which a corporation is capable of communicating to its audience its own capacity to act strategically can . . . determine its success in the marketplace. Ultimately, a company creates its own value by instilling a sense of confidence in its investors.[2]

These observations by Geraldine U. Foster, Senior Vice President, Investor Relations and Corporate Communications, Schering-Plough

Corporation, appeared in the Foreword to *The Search for Corporate Strategic Credibility: Concepts and Cases in Global Strategy Communications.* This commentary offers a useful historical perspective concerning the recent evolution of investor relations. It also provides an appropriate introduction to a discussion of the current state of investor relations— practice and theory—the subject of this chapter. In the pages that follow, we shall look at a number of major forces that have impacted the historical evolution of investor relations and continue to shape current practice today. A combination of institutional, global, and technological factors have influenced both the evolution and the current state of investor relations practice.

We shall also review a number of research studies that have explored the consequences associated with the practice of more active and open corporate strategic and financial communications. As the payoffs and pitfalls of an activist investor relations approach continue to be documented and more widely disseminated, we can anticipate further corporate interest in achieving the positive benefits (while minimizing the downside risks) involved in strategic and financial communications. This heightened corporate self-interest can, in turn, be expected to further shape the evolution of the investor relations function.

MAJOR FORCES:
INSTITUTIONALIZATION OF U.S. MARKETS

The Employment Retirement Income Security Act (ERISA), crafted by Congress in 1974, triggered the institutionalization of U.S. equity markets. By establishing procedures for governing private pension and benefit plans, Congress opened the door for the emergence of pension funds, in 1996 the single largest category of institutional investor. "The asset holdings of institutional investors as of the second quarter of 1996 topped $11.1 trillion."[3] Pension funds own the largest share of these holdings—46.8 percent.[4] Mutual funds and insurance company investment holdings have surged in recent years, to add to the institutionalization of U.S. equity markets.

The consequences for the practice of investor relations have been profound. Because of the legal fiduciary responsibilities to their clients, these institutions have demanded detailed and timely strategic and financial information. They have successfully sought an activist role in corporate governance, focusing their institutional power on company performance, the proper role of the board of directors, and executive compensation. Investor relations managers must now pay equal attention to the "buy side" as well as the "sell side." They must know the type of institution investing in their company. They must know their institutional investor's philosophy, their goals, and various investment strategies and techniques. They must determine what information should be disclosed, when, to whom, and how (channels of communication to be used), to an increasingly sophisticated and demanding body of institutional and individual investors. The overall impact of the institutionalization of U.S. equity markets has been to make the job of the investor relations executive infinitely more challenging and complex.

GLOBALIZATION OF CAPITAL MARKETS

As transnational corporations seek equity capital beyond their own domestic borders in order to fuel the global expansion of their businesses, the globalization of capital markets proceeds at a quickening pace:

Capital flows across national borders in two ways: as investment flows and as international trade financing. . . . At the end of 1996, U.S. holdings of foreign equities stood at more than $559 billion. The implication for investor relations is that U.S. companies are finding themselves in competition with non-U.S. companies for U.S. investor dollars, whether or not they choose to participate in an international investor relations effort. Competition for foreign investors, in concert with globalization of product markets, have obligated investor relations departments in U.S.-based corporations to delegate resources to international investor relations efforts.[5]

This, in turn, has added further complexity to the job of investor relations executives as their investor base becomes increasingly heterogeneous. Gaining familiarity with "foreign" capital markets presents challenges to non–U.S. and U.S. companies alike as they expand their participation in global capital markets. In Chapter 4 we will explore in greater depth the challenges of global strategic communications.

TECHNOLOGY

Technology continues to have a profound impact on the practice of investor relations. It has facilitated and helped to drive the institutionalization as well as the globalization of capital markets. Technology has led to round-the-clock trading and automated securities trading, and contributed to an efficient foreign-exchange marketplace.[6] Instantaneous access to the latest corporate strategic and financial information has altered both the transmission and the reception of investor relations communications. A more informed, sophisticated investor audience can be reached by companies with an arsenal of communications technology tools, including conference calls, the Internet, and e-mail, among others. In Chapter 5 we will report in greater detail on the use of these technology tools in the transmission and reception of strategic and financial information.

EVOLUTION OF THE INVESTOR RELATIONS FUNCTION

Investor relations has come a long way in a relatively brief period of time. In slightly more than ten years the investor relations function has evolved from a rather passive messenger of corporate financial information, primarily delivered to the Wall Street brokerage community, to that of a proactive, strategic marketer to giant institutional investors, as well as to smaller, individual investors. Even more recently, we are beginning to see an expansion of the IR role to include the management of corporate assets and shareholder value.

Investor relations has moved from a primarily passive, one-way communication role to an active—indeed, interactive—marketing function. In this evolving marketing role, investor relations serves as a link between the company and the investment community, responding to the needs of both. A perceived need to educate as well as inform internal company management and the external investment community is also part of this expanded marketing role. According to one investor relations officer,

The function IR officers serve is a conduit between our shareholders and our internal constituency, our senior management. It's my role to position the company, to inform, to educate and to serve. And that role goes both ways. As we look externally to our investors, be they institutional investors or individual investors, we look to position the company and inform them [investors] about key products, key events, strategy—providing financial details to support that—in an open and even manner. Internally, it's equally important to understand and to bring in the views of external constituents and share those with management.[7]

In the words of one global-equity portfolio manager, "The IR professional must be responsive to the needs of the corporation, on the one hand, and the needs of the investor on the other, and . . . savvy enough to understand both."[8]

In order to function effectively in this expanded marketing role, providing service and value to the company and market investors, the investor relations officer must be an integral part of management's "inner circle" and part of the "information loop." This means that the IR executive must be involved, actively engaged, and a full participant with senior management in the strategic activities and initiatives of the company. This accomplishes two things: (1) It provides the IR manager with a strategic perspective, as well as a source of strategic information to be shared, as appropriate, with the investment community; and (2) it assures access to and influence with senior management, as the IR officer provides relevant market information input to the strategic planning process. As the senior vice president of a securities company observed, "The best IR people I've found are those who are really in the inner circle . . . when the IR person is in the information loop, they're absolutely invaluable."[9]

To be a successful marketer, the IR officer needs to walk an exceedingly narrow path. As many marketing executives have discovered to their chagrin, overselling and overpromotion, whatever the product or service, can have serious, negative consequences. It's a fine line between being proactive and being overly promotional. As one analyst observed, "You don't want to be restrained and restricted in the information flow, but you also don't want to be glib and self-serving either. There has to be the right balance to add value to an investor community and hopefully to the stock price."[10]

These evolutionary developments have resulted in increased influence, responsibility, credibility, and significance for the investor relations function. An analyst commented as follows on the expanded role of IR: "It's my perspective that one reason the IR function has grown so important is the immediacy of information. . . . You need IR people to assist in that information flow. . . . On top of this, take a look at some of the larger companies, like General Electric, which is something like 2 per cent of real GDP. Investor relations for a company like that . . . is a tremendous service to the community at large, particularly the financial community."[11]

Along with increased responsibility comes a significant increase in the complexity of the IR task. One investor relations officer observed, "The IR field is getting more and more complex. It's a lot more than just putting out a press release and then talking to a couple of people. I look at it in terms of segments that I serve, individual segments, the institutional segment, which breaks into the buy side and the sell side, then there's the sell-side and buy-side analysts and the portfolio managers, all of whom have diverse information needs. Then add to that overseas investors."[12]

In addition to increased responsibility and complexity, opportunities for an even more expanded IR role are emerging—a chance to become an active partner in the management of corporate assets and shareholder value, as mentioned earlier. According to one investor and public relations manager, "The opportunity now presents itself for investor relations officers to bring new ideas forward to internal management on how value can be unleashed. Progressive investor relations calls for a new role for IR officers as internal sell-side analysts, shopping strategic moves, such as mergers and acquisitions (M&A) and spin-off ideas to management."[13]

What have been the consequences of a collision between a more demanding, sophisticated investment community and a more proactive, responsive IR marketing approach—both sides armed with the latest in communications technology? Clearly, the investment community has emerged as a major beneficiary. As the result of the impact of forces such as the institutionalization and globalization of capital markets, advances in communications technology, and the evolution of a more progressive IR function, the character and content of strategic communications and the disclosure of strategic information is changing. As noted earlier, the process is becoming more open and candid and information is becoming more specific, timely, and forward looking. As one analyst observed, "As far as being candid, there's absolutely no question about it. The equilibrium of a stock price is there because of the openness of the information, the candor of management and its willingness to be subject to the disciplines of the marketplace."[14] According to Theodore Pincus, chairman and managing partner of the Financial Relations Board, the country's largest investor relations firm, "A new era of 'corporate glasnost' is steadily emerging. The past year has witnessed an unprecedented increase in the frequency and depth of forward-looking investor communications by both large and small cap public companies."[15]

But what about companies? Have they reaped any benefits from this so-called new era of corporate glasnost? What have been the corporate consequences of all these evolutionary changes in the role of IR and the character and content of communications and disclosure? Considerable research has been conducted in recent years examining these questions. The following section examines some of the results of this research, findings that show that substantial company benefits can be achieved from more open and progressive investor relations practices.

BENEFITS OF OPEN AND CANDID STRATEGIC COMMUNICATIONS

Compelling evidence is rapidly accumulating about significant tangible and intangible benefits associated with open and candid strategic communications. Positive payoffs include increased coverage by security analysts (more analysts following the company), increased accuracy in earnings forecasts, an increase in interest among investors, increased liquidity of stocks, and a lower cost of capital.

Lang and Lundholm found a direct link between the openness of a company's strategic communications and the number of analysts following the firm, their accuracy in forecasting annual earnings per share, a consensus among analysts in their EPS forecasts, and the volatility of their forecast revisions during the fiscal year.[16] (The more open a company's disclosure of information, the greater the number of analysts following the firm and the more accurate their EPS forecasts.) A larger, better-informed analyst following, with greater confidence in a company's future prospects, tends to attract the attention and interest of an increasing number of investors. Dhaliwal found similar results regarding the relationship between open disclosure and the size of an analyst's following.[17] Dhaliwal also found a link between information disclosure and greater investor interest, while Eccles and Mavrinac found a relationship between improved corporate disclosure and the number of "patient investors" attracted to a company's shareholder base.[18] Dhaliwal, Diamond and Verrechia, Elliott and Jacobson, and Lev all have found a connection between disclosure and the cost of equity capital.[19] With analysts and investors in possession of more accurate, timely, and forward-looking strategic and financial information, uncertainty and the perception of risk are reduced (reducing the premium demanded as a hedge against risk and uncertainty), thereby effectively lowering the cost of capital.

Empirical evidence of a positive relationship between strategic communications, open disclosure, and share price is less compelling, although some does exist. In addition, anecdotal evidence and qualitative surveys have suggested the existence of such a bond. In a study of health-care companies, the author and associates discovered a relationship between the quality of corporate financial communications, as measured by the Financial Analysts Federation's annual evaluation of corporate communications and price/earnings (P/E) multiples for the period 1984–1987.[20] In this study we found a statistically significant correlation between quality of financial communications and price/earnings multiples. Those firms that scored higher in evaluations by the Financial Analysts Federation enjoyed a greater increase in P/E multiples over a three-year period, as compared with companies rated lower in their financial communications.

Also, in Chapter 2 we reported the results of a test of our strategic credibility model, which showed that high-credibility companies achieved higher market/book price ratios than low-credibility companies. Inasmuch as strategic communications was the second most significant determinant of strategic credibility, presumably part of the higher M/B ratios was the result of communications.

There appears to be no shortage of qualitative studies—many of which involve CEO perceptions—concerning the benefits of strategic communications and investor relations. It turns out that improved share price is perceived by chief executive officers as one of the most significant payoffs. In a study of CEOs of the top 250 nonbanking public companies in Florida, Petersen and Martin reported that "increasing stock prices" was one of the important results of investor relations, at least according to the executives included in their study.[21] In a study of corporate managers, financial analysts, and investors, Eccles and

Mavrinac found that "increased credibility" and "increased share value" were the two most significant potential benefits associated with improvements and investments in investor relations.[22]

Anecdotal evidence abounds concerning the link between corporate strategic communications and share price. United Technologies in aerospace, the Chesapeake Corp. in the paper industry, and the Allen Group in auto replacement parts all were believed to be rewarded for their strategic candor by favorable price/earnings multiples.[23] As reported in *The Search for Corporate Strategic Credibility*,

Air Products and Chemicals, Inc., with an intensive and effective effort to communicate its strategy to key stakeholders, leveraged a sound strategic vision, and, in the process, enhanced its shareholder value. Largely as the result of a three-year, $200,000 corporate strategy communications program, Air Products' P/E multiple increased four times faster than the Standard and Poors' 500. From a 23% discount in 1989, the company's stock was trading at a 3% premium in 1992. Stock market value increased 100% or $2.5 billion during the three-year period.[24]

CONCLUSION

World-class strategic communications companies are in the forefront of progressive investor relations practices. As a general rule, they tend to anticipate rather than react to basic forces such as the institutionalization and globalization of capital markets. They tend to be pioneers in the development and use of advanced technologies, but they view these technologies as means to an end, as tools to leverage their progressive investor relations practices, not as ends in themselves. The evolution of the IR function has proceeded further and faster in these leading companies, moving from messengers of financial information, to marketers of corporate equities, to asset managers and collaborators in the process of shareholder creation.

The job of the investor relations officer in these companies has become more complex, interactive, strategic, significant, and responsible. IR executives occupy a place at the table, the "inner loop" and "inside circle," regularly participating in the strategic affairs and initiatives of their companies.

Strategic communications in world-class IR companies have become more candid, specific, timely, and future oriented, which has allowed them to reap the benefits and payoffs of open disclosure while minimizing the costs and downside risks. This has meant a lower cost of capital, improved liquidity, and a larger and better-informed analyst following, which, in turn, has attracted an increased number of patient investors. In the long run this can only lead to an improved share price and an enhancement of shareholder value.

Figure 3.1
The Evolution of Investor Relations: Theory and Practice

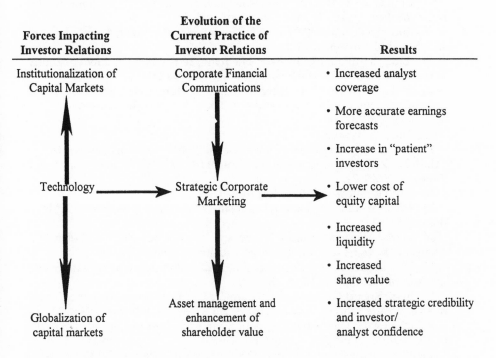

Forces Impacting Investor Relations	Evolution of the Current Practice of Investor Relations	Results
Institutionalization of Capital Markets	Corporate Financial Communications	• Increased analyst coverage
		• More accurate earnings forecasts
		• Increase in "patient" investors
Technology	Strategic Corporate Marketing	• Lower cost of equity capital
		• Increased liquidity
		• Increased share value
Globalization of capital markets	Asset management and enhancement of shareholder value	• Increased strategic credibility and investor/ analyst confidence

In Part II of the book we will meet six of these companies: AT&T, Schering-Plough Corporation, Reuters PLC, BASF, Sony, and Toyota Motors Corporation.

In Figure 3.1 there is a conceptual scheme that summarizes the major forces that affect the evolution of the investor relations function and the benefits and payoffs of open disclosure and candid strategic communications.

NOTES

1. Excerpts of a review by Louis M. Thompson, Jr., President and CEO, National Investor Relations Institute, which appeared on the cover of Richard B. Higgins, *The Search for Corporate Strategic Credibility: Concepts and Cases in Global Strategy Communications* (Westport, Conn.: Quorum Books, 1996).

2. Ibid., from the Foreword by Geraldine U. Foster, xiii, xiv.

3. Geraldine U. Foster, "IR Today: The Changing Environment of Investor Relations," *Investor Relations Quarterly* 1 (Summer 1997): 5.

4. Ibid.

5. Ibid., 10, 11, 12–13.

6. Ibid., 13–14.

7. Constance K. Weaver, "IRQ Roundtable: Life With or Without IR," *Investor Relations Quarterly* 1 (Summer 1997): 62.

8. Ibid., 76 (Thomas P. Moore, Jr., Senior Vice President, State Street Research and Management Co.).

9. Ibid., 76 (Julianne C. Iwerson-Niemann, Senior Vice President of Equity Research and Portfolio Management, Huntleigh Securities).

10. Ibid., 76 (Kevin C. Murphy, Principal at Morgan Stanley and Co. and presently the analyst in charge of the airline and air freight industries).

11. Ibid., 78 (Murphy).

12. Ibid., 73 (Weaver).

13. Bradley D. Allen, Director, Investor and Public Relations, Imation Corp., "The New Sell Side: The Strategic Direction of IR," *Investor Relations Quarterly* 1 (Summer 1997): 21.

14. "IRQ Roundtable," 65 (Murphy).

15. Theodore Pincus, "Full(er) Disclosure," *Reputation Management* 3 (May/ June 1997): 30.

16. Mark Lang and Russell J. Lundholm, "Corporate Disclosure Policy and Analyst Behavior," *Accounting Review* 1 (October 1996): 467–492.

17. D. S. Dhaliwal, "Disclosure Regulations and the Cost of Capital," *Southern Economic Journal* 45 (1979): 785–794.

18. Ibid.; Robert G. Eccles and Sarah C. Mavrinac, "Improving the Corporate Disclosure Process," *Sloan Management Review* 36 (Summer 1995): 23.

19. Dhaliwal, "Disclosure Regulations and the Cost of Capital," 785–794; D. W. Diamond and R. E. Verrechia, "Disclosure, Liquidity and the Cost of Capital," *Journal of Finance* 66 (1991): 1325–1359; R. K. Elliott and P. D. Jacobson, "Costs and Benefits of Business Information Disclosure," *Accounting Horizons* 8, no. 4 (1994): 80–96; Baruch Lev, "Information Disclosure Strategy," *California Management Review* 34 (Summer 1992): 9–29.

20. Richard B. Higgins and Brendan D. Bannister, "Corporate Communications: 'Frontrunners' vs. 'Challengers,'" in *1989/1990 Handbook of Business Strategy*, ed. Harold E. Glass (Boston: Warren, Gorham and Lamont, 1990), 1–7.

21. Barbara K. Petersen and Hugh J. Martin, "CEO Perceptions of the IR Function: An Exploratory Study," *Investor Relations Quarterly* 1 (Summer 1997): 43.

22. Eccles and Mavrinac, "Improving the Corporate Disclosure Process," 23.

23. Theodore Pincus, "How to Boost Your P/E Multiple," *Fortune*, 10 November 1986.

24. Higgins, *Search for Corporate Strategic Credibility*, xxiii.

4

Global Strategy Communications

Three powerful forces have converged to have a profound impact on the conduct, quality, and texture of corporate strategic and financial communications in the 1990s: The institutionalization and globalization of capital markets and the explosion and rapid advances in communications technology.[1] The institutionalization of capital markets has generated inexorable pressures for more open, detailed, and candid disclosure of strategic and financial information. Institutional investors, sophisticated in financial matters and politically powerful in ways that individual investors never have been, have opened up access to hitherto well-guarded corporate information and decision-making processes. Institutional investors have turned up the heat on corporate governance issues and opened up the valves (if not the floodgates) controlling open disclosure of information of corporate performance and future strategic intent.[2] The long-lasting effects have yet to fully unfold, but they will undoubtedly influence "traditional" notions of shareholder capitalism for generations to come.

The globalization of capital markets has served to transmit this increasing openness of corporate strategic and financial information on a worldwide scale and, in the process, encourage trends toward uniformity in corporate communications and investor relations practices.[3] These trends, first observed in the United States, are picking up steam and are proceeding at an increasingly brisk pace in Japan and Europe.[4] Movement toward global regulatory requirements and common accounting standards have further contributed to a thrust toward more open communications and disclosure.[5] The achievement of complete global uniformity in investor relations may never occur, but make no mistake about it, momentum is building in this direction.

If the institutionalization and globalization of capital markets are providing pressures for increased openness in corporate strategic and financial communications, technology is providing a powerful tool to allow this to happen. Worldwide acceptance and application of the Internet, e-mail, conference calls, and other advances in communications technology is providing instantaneous access to corporate strategic and financial information unheard of only ten years ago. It also magnifies the movement toward the institutionalization and globalization of capital markets and accelerates these trends at an exponentially increasing rate.

TWO GLOBAL STRATEGY COMMUNICATION SURVEYS

Conventional wisdom suggests that the globalization of capital markets will encourage an international uniformity in investor relations practices. More specifically, globalization will cause a convergence in financial communications attitudes and behavior. Reasons given for this convergence include the imposition of uniform regulatory requirements (the SEC, for example) and the growing acceptance of common accounting standards (GAP accounting, for example).

In 1993 a survey of investor relations executives and security analysts in the United States, Europe, and Japan revealed significant differences in strategic communications practices among these three countries/regions and between IR executives, as a group, and security analysts in all three areas.[6] In many if not most cases, U.S. and European responses tracked together quite closely, with significant differences showing up between the United States–Europe and Japan. As a general rule, respondents reported that U.S.–European companies were more open and timely in their strategic communications than Japanese corporations. Differences between all executives and all analysts must be interpreted with caution due to the relatively low return rate and distribution of responses from security analysts.

Predictably, perhaps, security analysts reported wider gaps (differences) between the amount of information that needs to be sent and the amount of information actually sent than company executives. Also, companies believed that the information they were sending was more timely than did analysts. Surprisingly, perhaps, U.S. investor relations executives reported that they were actually sending less information than needed to be sent.

While U.S. executives (and U.S. and European analysts) reported negative gaps between the amount of information actually provided and information needed, Japanese executives saw very little discrepancy between the amount of information needed and information actually sent. Japanese analysts reported only a slight negative difference. In another cross-cultural comparison, U.S. and European executives believed that their communications were more timely than did their Japanese counterparts.

Japanese respondents (executives and analysts) believed that Japanese companies take too little credit for good performance—as compared to U.S. and European executives and analysts. However, U.S. and European executives rated their companies as being more open and specific in their communications about past performances and future strategies. Security analysts in all three regions rated companies as being less open and specific in providing information about past performance and future strategies than did company executives.

European and Japanese executives believed that their companies had developed effective global strategies, while U.S. executives were less positive in assessments of their companies' global strategies. Global strategy effectiveness was evaluated according to three criteria:[7]

- Does the company achieve worldwide economies of scale?
- Does the strategy effectively respond to national or local differences?
- Does the company have a worldwide learning capability that results in high levels of product, process and organizational innovation?

1998 UPDATE

In 1998 this same survey was replicated among investor relations executives only (security analysts were omitted due to their low response rate in 1993). Questionnaires were mailed to 790 investor relations executives. The response rate to the 1998 survey was 17.2 percent, slightly less than the 17.9-percent rate of IR executives in 1993. Again, we gratefully acknowledge the support of the Investor Relations Institutes and Associations in the United States, the United Kingdom, France, Germany, and Japan for their assistance in mailing and collecting questionnaires from their members. Also, we wish to thank Professor Constantine Spiliotes and his student, Louisa Serene, both of Dartmouth College, for their invaluable help in tabulating and analyzing the questionnaire data.

The purpose of the 1998 survey was twofold: In general, to provide a five-year update to our earlier survey and to determine what changes, if any, had occurred in strategic communications attitudes and behavior in the United States, the United Kingdom, France, Germany, and Japan in the interim period; and, more specifically, to test the following hypotheses:

Hypothesis #1

As the globalization of capital markets proceeds, country and regional differences in investor relations practices and attitudes toward corporate strategic and financial communications will tend to diminish. This trend toward convergence in worldwide communications attitudes and practices will continue as capital markets continue to globalize.

Hypothesis #2

Overall, the level of openness, timeliness, and specificity in corporate strategic and financial communications will increase as institutional and market forces compel more open disclosure. These forces will tend to countervail, and gradually overcome, the influence of cultural forces that tend to discourage more open communications.

RESULTS

Continuing Differences in Practices

Table 4.1 presents mean averages for a number of communication variables. The list that follows explains the symbol terminology used:

Table 4.1
Mean Averages: 1993 versus 1998 (by Country)

	1993			1998		
Variable	United States	Japan	Europe	United States	Japan	Europe
SOUR 2	3.45	3.12	3.22	3.31	3.22	3.39
SOUR 3	3.64	3.13	3.59	3.50	3.21	3.82
DEC 1	2.90	2.86	3.07	3.05	3.17	3.24
DEC 2	3.21	2.86	3.17	3.23	3.29	3.26
DEC 3	3.63	3.07	3.71	3.66	3.33	3.80
FUTUNCER	3.77	3.48	3.80	3.68	3.88	4.00
PASTOPEN	4.29	3.73	4.07	4.18	4.09	4.28
PASTSPEC	3.86	3.36	3.69	3.80	3.58	3.85
ATTRIB	2.95	3.45	2.98	3.04	3.60	3.11
GLOBSTR	3.31	3.54	3.70	3.31	3.36	3.94

SOUR 2—Amount of information we need to send, all sources.[8] 1 = very little; 5 = very great.

SOUR 3—Timeliness of information sent, all sources. 1 = very untimely; 5 = very timely.

DEC 1—Amount of information we actually send, all decisions. 1 = very little; 5 = very great.

DEC 2—Amount of information we need to send, all decisions. 1 = very little; 5 = very great.

DEC 3—Timeliness of information sent, all decisions. 1 = very untimely; 5 = very timely.

FUTUNCER—Communications reduce future uncertainty. 1 = strongly disagree; 5 = strongly agree.

PASTOPEN—Communications about past performance are quite open. 1 = strongly disagree; 5 = strongly agree.

PASTSPEC—Communications about past performance are quite specific. 1 = strongly disagree; 5 = strongly agree.

ATTRIB—Company takes too little credit for good performance, accepting blame for poor performance. 1 = strongly disagree; 5 = strongly agree.

GLOBSTR—Overall effectiveness of company's global strategy. 1 = very ineffective; 5 = very effective.

Averages for the United States, Europe, and Japan are shown for both 1993 and 1998. It should be noted that all of these communications

Table 4.2
Differences of Means: Levels of Statistical Significance (1998)

Variable	United States versus Europe	United States versus Japan	Europe versus Japan
SOUR 2	—	—	—
SOUR 3	—	0.008	0.000
DEC 1	—	—	—
DEC 2	—	—	—
DEC 3	—	0.003	0.001
FUTUNCER	0.047	0.040	—
PASTOPEN	—	—	—
PASTSPEC	—	—	0.050
ATTRIB	—	0.000	0.000
GLOBSTR	—	—	0.012

Note: No value indicates no statistical significance among differences.

variables showed statistically significant differences among countries/regions in 1993. As Table 4.2 indicates, six of these ten variables continue to show statistically significant differences in 1998.

SOUR 3 and DEC 3—U.S. and European executives continue to believe that their companies provide more timely information from "all sources" and "for all decisions" than did Japanese executives.

FUTUNCER—According to respondents, European and Japanese companies provide more information about future strategies than U.S. companies. It should be noted that this represents a dramatic turnaround from 1993, with Japan and Europe showing significant increases in "future uncertainty reduction," while the United States showed a decline.

PASTSPEC—European executives continue to believe that their companies provide more specific communications about past performance than their U.S. and Japanese counterparts.

ATTRIB—Japanese respondents continued to report that Japanese companies take too little credit for good performance, as compared to U.S. and European executives.

GLOBSTR—Japanese executives continue to believe that their companies have developed effective global strategies, while U.S. and European executives were less positive in assessments of their companies' global strategies.

Convergence in IR Practices

Table 4.2 also shows convergence in financial communication practices in a number of areas, including SOUR 2, DEC 1, DEC 2, and PASTOPEN. In each of these cases, practices that showed statistically significant differences among countries/regions in 1993 no longer were statistically significant in 1998.

No longer did IR executives in the United States, Japan, and Europe report significant differences in the "amount of information that we need to send, all sources" (SOUR 2), the "amount of information we actually send, all decisions" (DEC 1), or in the "amount of information we need to send, all decisions" (DEC 2). Also converging were communication practices regarding openness about past performance (PASTOPEN).

While some of the diminishing differences among countries/regions occurred as the result of declines by the United States (SOUR 2 and PASTOPEN) from 1993 to 1998, as Table 4.2 shows rather dramatically, the convergence in communications practices was due primarily to reported increases in openness in Japanese IR communications.

Overall Increases in Openness, Specificity, and Timeliness

Table 4.3 shows combined mean averages, computed by averaging the mean values for the United States, Japan, and Europe for 1993 and

Table 4.3
Mean Averages: United States, Japan, Europe

Variable	1993	1998	Difference
SOUR 2	3.30	3.31	.01
SOUR 3	3.49	3.50	.01
DEC 1	2.94	3.16	.22*
DEC 2	3.11	3.26	.15**
DEC 3	3.53	3.59	.06
FUTUNCER	3.71	3.86	.15
PASTOPEN	4.10	4.18	.08
PASTSPEC	3.69	3.74	.05
ATTRIB	3.06	3.27	.21*
GLOBSTR	3.51	3.55	.04

*Statistically significant at the 0.01 level.
**Statistically significant at the 0.10 level.

again for 1998. These composite averages for each of the ten communications variables provide comparative measures of the overall openness, timeliness, and specificity of corporate strategic and financial communications in 1993 versus 1998. In comparing 1998 mean values with 1993 averages, it should be noted that larger numbers represent higher levels of openness, timeliness, and specificity, due to the scale construction of our questionnaire.

While each communication variable shows some increase in 1998 versus 1993, in several of the cases the increases are almost negligible and certainly not statistically significant. In the case of DEC 1, DEC 2, FUTUNCER, and ATTRIB, however, the increases are more substantial, showing a trend toward overall greater openness in corporate strategic and financial communications (as well as an increasing willingness in all three countries/regions for companies to accept blame for poor performance) (see Figure 4.1 for a graph of significant differences).

Table 4.4 presents comparative data, by country/region, regarding general attitudes toward strategy communications for 1993 and 1998. Although substantial differences first reported in 1993 continued to

Figure 4.1
Significant Differences, Mean Averages (All Countries, 1993 versus 1998)

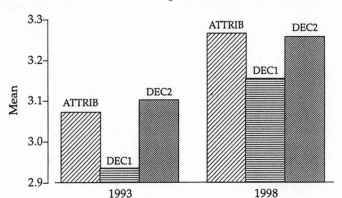

exist in 1998, convergence in attitudes among countries/regions also can be seen, perhaps most dramatically in response to question 2 (It is best for companies to detail the specifics of their strategic plans). While U.S. and European executives continued to remain skeptical of this proposition, Japanese executives responding favorably to this notion (either "agree" or "strongly agree") increased from 39 percent in 1993 to 73 percent in 1998. Smaller but similar increases on the part of Japanese IR executives also contributed to convergence of attitudes in question 4 (Talking openly about the past, present, and future is the best communication policy for a company to take), where Japanese favorability ratings increased from 68 percent in 1993 to 85 percent in 1998. Again, in comparing percentages for the three countries/regions for 1993 versus 1998, there appears to be a trend toward greater openness, timeliness, and specificity in corporate strategic and financial communications.

DISCUSSION AND ANALYSIS

Convergence in global corporate strategic communications occurred largely as the result of significant increases in open communications on the part of Japanese companies, at least according to the responses of IR executives included in our survey. This came as a rather unexpected result, given earlier findings obtained in our 1993 survey. Why this reported change in Japanese investor relations practices? According to Yoshiko Sato, program director and senior research fellow of the Japan Investor Relations Association (JIRA), several factors may have accounted for this turnaround:

Table 4.4
General Attitudes toward Strategy Communications: Investor Relations
Executive Responses (Percentages of Respondents Answering "Agree" or
"Strongly Agree")

Variable	1993			1998		
	U.S.	Japan	Europe	U.S.	Japan	Europe
1. It is best for companies to keep the financial community aware of their strategic plans.	94.7%	78.6	95.8	97.6	83.3	95.7
2. It is best for companies to detail the specifics of their strategic plans.	49.1	39.3	37.5	52.4	72.9	58.7
3. It does not put a company at a competitive disadvantage to openly discuss its strategic plans.	54.4	35.7	52.1	52.4	37.5	63.0
4. Talking openly about the past, present and future is the best communication policy for a company to take.	87.7	67.9	97.9	83.3	85.4	97.8
5. Timely, accurate communications increases the strategic credibility of a company.	93.0	96.4	97.9	97.6	100.0	95.7

- Japanese corporations have been forced to become more efficient [in] considering ROE and other related ratios. [Until recently, most Japanese companies felt little or no compulsion to disclose information about corporate strategy or financial performance. Enjoying a close relationship with banks more than willing and able to provide funds for capital investment, Japanese corporations have been sheltered from shareholder demands for information about strategic direction and corporate performance. With increasing reliance on equity capital as a source of capital funding, Japanese companies are discovering some of the realities of free-market capitalism. One such reality is pressure to provide open and timely strategic and financial information to investors and members of the investment community. Another reality is the need to pay attention to investor concerns such as share price and ROE.]

- A sharp decline in share price and [decline] of ratings [have given] a shock to top management. Attendance of top management [at] IR activities has risen sharply from last year [1997].
- Changes in the accounting system and deregulation have affected the Japanese corporate culture.

As a reflection of the increased importance of investor relations as a corporate activity in Japan,

Directors in charge of IR activities have been shifted to senior levels . . . from the general manager [level] in 1993 to the managing director [level] in 1998. Also, it is noteworthy that the attendance of top management increased this year [1998]. For example, the presence of top management [at] information meetings for analysts and institutional investors increased to 61.6 percent in 1998. . . . Comparing this figure with 1997 . . . which was 27.4 percent, it rose by more than double.[9]

It should be noted that the increased openness in Japanese investor relations and communication practices in the past five years coincides closely with the founding and development of the Japan Investor Relations Association, created in 1993. It is also interesting to note that 1993 coincided with our first global strategy communications survey, a study that revealed significant differences in U.S.–Europe and Japanese IR practices. Convergence in global IR practices can be attributed (at least partially) to active programs at JIRA and other national investor relations and security analyst associations designed to raise the consciousness level of companies concerning the need for more open and candid financial communications. This, combined with external pressures generated by institutional investors and globalization of capital markets, is clearly having an impact on worldwide corporate strategic and financial communications.

Convergence in IR activities was also created, to a lesser extent, by a decline in openness in some countries, particularly the United States. Although not as dramatic as Japanese increases, a wariness of U.S. companies to disclose detailed financial information, particularly regarding predictions of future performance, can be attributed to the chill resulting from a rash of shareholder lawsuits filed against companies that failed to meet expected levels of performance.

The gradual process of "thawing out" appears to be well underway, however, in the opinion of some:

It is now more than a year since President Clinton signed into law the Private Securities Litigation Reform Act of 1995, which provided corporations with a "safe harbor" for forward-looking statements in an attempt to reduce the number of lawsuits against companies whose financial communications fell short of estimates. In the past year, the climate for financial communications has changed dramatically as CEOs have demonstrated a newfound willingness to share information with their shareholders.[10]

Nevertheless, there still appears to be a ways to go before the ice melts completely, a condition known as "iceout" by our friends in Northern New England. As noted earlier, U.S. corporate communications designed to reduce future uncertainty took a precipitous decline in 1998 from 1993, in sharp contrast to increases in communications regarding future strategies reported in Europe and Japan. Apparently the chill still lingers, as evidenced by the findings presented and a number of open-ended comments provided by respondents to our 1998 survey. In response to our question, "What can be done to reduce cultural barriers to more open strategy communications," one U.S. investor relations manager said, "A better understanding of 'safe harbor' provisions may allow more companies to disclose more forward-looking information. *Legal counsel needs to more fully understand and appreciate this need* [emphasis added]." Another U.S. investor relations executive muttered, perhaps with tongue in cheek (and perhaps not), "Downsize legal departments."

Offsetting these less-than-optimistic views of convergence, a number of other investor relations officers commented in a more positive way. A U.S. investor relations executive said, "U.S. standards of disclosure are now the norm worldwide. . . . Disseminating information is the real challenge." A German IR director offered, "Today we don't see major cultural barriers anymore since . . . communication within the financial community is nearly [completely] globally harmonized," and an executive from Japan stated, "It is becoming a common rule to meet . . . ISO standards to have some base for quality and environmental issues."

GLOBAL STRATEGY COMMUNICATIONS
SCOREBOARD, 1998

The following list reports on our most recent evaluation of leading global strategy communications corporations in the United States, Europe, and Japan. Investor relations executives were asked to identify the top five companies in strategy communications in the United States, Europe, and Japan. As the list indicates, Coca-Cola, followed closely by General Electric, led all U.S. companies. In Europe, Daimler-

Benz was a clear winner, while in Japan, Sony again emerged as the number-one strategy communications company by a wide margin.[11]

United States		Europe		Japan	
Coca-Cola	23	Daimler-Benz	18	Sony	28
General Electric	21	Novartis	8	Toyota	13
Microsoft	16	Hoechst	6	Honda	12
IBM	11	Nestle	6	Ito-Yokado	6
Citicorp	8	Philips	6	Mitsubishi	6

It should be noted that both Sony and Daimler-Benz are listed on the New York Stock Exchange (NYSE), probably more than a coincidence, given their impressive records in open corporate information communications.[12]

SUMMARY AND CONCLUSIONS

While differences in communication practices among countries and regions continue to exist in 1998, significant convergence has also occurred in the past five years with several communications variables. It appears that Japanese IR communications, at least as reported by respondents in our survey, have substantially contributed to this convergence. Increased openness, timeliness, and specificity in Japanese financial communications practices also appear to have contributed to an overall increase in openness, timeliness, and specificity in global corporate financial communications in 1998.

Whether this trend toward convergence and increased openness, timeliness, and specificity in corporate strategic and financial communications will continue is difficult to predict with any certainty. Global recession, military conflict, and any number of unforeseen circumstances could interrupt movement toward global prosperity and continuing globalization of capital markets. Lacking such calamitous events, however, it seems reasonable to assume that trends toward convergence and increasing openness, timeliness, and specificity, well underway for at least the past five years, will continue well past the millennium. In the words of Calpers President William Crist, "Globalization [and convergence—our insertion] is inexorable. No one could stop it even if they wanted to."[13]

NOTES

1. Michael Unseem, "Corporate Leadership in a Globalizing Equity Market," *Academy of Management Executive* 12 (November 1998): 44–45.
2. See California Public Employees' Retirement System, *Calpers Adopts In-*

ternational Governance Program (Sacramento: California Public Employees Retirement System, 1996). See also J. Cossette, "Making Waves," *Investor Relations* (October 1997): 27–31.

3. R. Lambert, "NYExchange Sees Wider Horizons," *Financial Times*, 24 September 1997, 4.

4. Japan Investor Relations Association, "Investor Relations Activities in Japan," *Tokyo Stock Exchange Magazine*, July 1998, 2–5.

5. Unseem, "Corporate Leadership," 49.

6. Richard B. Higgins, *The Search for Corporate Strategic Credibility: Concepts and Cases in Global Strategy Communications* (Westport, Conn.: Quorum Books, 1996), 131–146.

7. These criteria were taken from Christopher A. Bartlett and Sumantra Ghoshal, *Managing Across Borders* (Boston: Harvard Business School Press, 1989).

8. "All sources" includes general press, annual reports, financial statements, general meetings (with security analysts), individual meetings, plant visits, clipping services, industry publications, government documents, and all others. "All decisions" includes joint venture formation, new R&D or capital expenditure programs, product development strategies, company acquisition announcements, new product announcements, quantitative predictions of future performance, warnings of negative events (e.g., earnings decline), explaining dividend increases, basic changes in strategy, and all others.

9. Japan Investor Relations Association, "Investor Relations Activities in Japan," 2, 3–4.

10. Theodore Pincus, "Full(er) Disclosure," *Reputation Management* 3 (May/June 1997): 30.

11. Twenty-three respondents included Coca-Cola among the top five corporations in the United States in strategy communications. Eighteen respondents included Daimler-Benz among the top five corporations in Europe in strategy communications. Twenty-eight respondents included Sony among the top five corporations in Japan in strategy communications.

12. Incidentally, there are currently twelve Japanese companies listed on the NYSE, with a number more planning or in the process of listing. Three companies, Amway Japan, NTT, and Orix, have listed since June 1994.

13. California Public Employees' Retirement System, *Calpers Adopts International Governance Program.*

5

The Use of Technology in Corporate Financial Communications

Too many investor relations Web sites simply republish information available elsewhere, often failing to take advantage of the
interactivity the new medium makes possible.[1]

Dramatic advances in communications technology are rapidly transforming the way companies provide strategic and financial information to the investment community. Conference calls, the Internet,
e-mail, and other technologies have the potential of providing more
timely, detailed, specific information, while also increasing the interactive communications possibilities among companies, investors, analysts, and others in the financial community.

The Securities and Exchange Commission has gone on record as
endorsing the Internet as an investor communications medium. In 1997
the SEC stated, "The use of electronic media enhances the efficiency of
securities markets by allowing for the rapid dissemination of information to investors and financial markets in a more cost-efficient, wide-
spread and equitable manner than traditional paper-based methods."[2]

Major advantages offered by the Internet include speed of distribution of a greater amount of unfiltered information and equal access
for individual and institutional shareholders. "Press releases . . . [can be
posted on corporate Internet Web sites as soon as the release has been
publicly disseminated to the wires], and electronic distribution of information enhances investors' ability to access, research and analyze information. Individual investors and indeed a wide range of stakeholders
can have access to timely information 24 hours a day."[3] Parentheti-

cally (and perhaps another reason for their endorsement of the Internet), the electronic distribution of information also enhances the SEC's ability to access, research, and analyze company information.

Is the potential for improving communications between companies and members of the investment community being fully exploited and effectively utilized? This chapter presents the results of two recent research projects undertaken to answer these and other questions.

In June 1996 the National Investor Relations Institute launched an ongoing survey research program designed "to measure the impact of technological change and track how corporate IR officers are using ever more sophisticated tools in communicating with the investment community. The goal is to provide guidance to NIRI members on an ongoing basis as they integrate new technologies into their IR programs."[4] In 1996 the Rivel Research Group surveyed a sample of NIRI's membership on key technology-related subjects. In a follow-on study in 1998, a total of 202 senior IR managers at NIRI corporate member firms were interviewed by telephone between February 4 and 20, again by the Rivel Research Group.

In the fall of 1998 the Association for Investment Management and Research, a professional association representing a global membership of investment professionals, worked with a consulting group, Stratcom Associates, to design a survey of AIMR members. A survey questionnaire was developed to determine the extent to which companies, regularly followed by members of AIMR, had adopted and were utilizing conference calls, the Internet, e-mail, and other technologies to provide information to the investment community. Analysts and portfolio managers were asked to evaluate these technologies as a source of strategic and financial information. They were also asked to rate the quality, timeliness, and specificity of information provided by companies. Suggestions for improvement in the utilization of various technologies were solicited, as well as analyst preferences in the use of specific technologies. The stated purpose of the results of this survey was "to educate corporate CFO's and Investor Relations Officers regarding the requirements and wishes of analysts who follow their companies."

The first mailing of questionnaires was sent to a sample of 2,000 analysts in October 1998, with a second follow-up mailing to these same analysts in November. Between the first and second mailings a total of 355 usable responses were received from AIMR members, a response rate of 17.8 percent. Of these 355 usable questionnaires, 56 percent of respondents were identified as buy-side analysts, 20 percent as portfolio managers, 8 percent as sell-side analysts, and 16 percent as other.

Taken together, these two surveys provide an opportunity to compare and contrast the utilization of recently developed communications technologies by the senders (companies) and the receivers (analysts) of corporate strategic and financial information. In addition, the AIMR survey provides companies with feedback regarding analysts' perceptions of the value, quality, timeliness, and specificity of information companies are making available through these new technologies. Finally, the results of the AIMR survey present companies with feedback from users regarding their preferences and suggestions for improvements in utilizing technology in the practice of investor relations.

RESULTS

Analysts' Conference Calls

In the AIMR study, 58 percent of analysts reported that "almost all" of the companies that they followed conduct analyst conference calls. Thirty-eight percent responded that "some" of the companies they followed conduct conference for analysts. Only 4 percent reported that "none" of the companies followed conduct analyst conference calls. In the NIRI study (1998), 83 percent of the companies surveyed reported that they conduct analyst conference calls.[5]

Of the three major technologies included in the AIMR survey (conference calls, the Internet, and e-mail), conference calls were rated by analysts as the most valuable source of strategic and financial information. Forty-seven percent of analysts reported that conference calls were a "very valuable" source; 48 percent said conference calls were "somewhat valuable"; while only 5 percent rated conference calls as "not valuable." On a 6-point scale, where 6 equals "extremely valuable" and 1 equals "not at all valuable," conference calls received a mean average rating from "all respondents" of 4.36. Breaking down mean average ratings by respondent position gives the following results: buy-side analysts equals 4.59, sell-side analysts equals 4.42, portfolio managers equals 4.09, and other equals 3.85.

All respondents rated the quality, timeliness, and specificity of strategic and financial information provided in analyst conference calls as superior to the information provided by either the Internet or e-mail. Thirty-five percent of analysts evaluated the quality as "good" or "outstanding"; 53 percent rated the timeliness of information provided in conference calls as "good" or "outstanding"; and 20 percent reported that the specificity of this information was "good" or "outstanding" (see Table 5.1). In terms of additional information desired from companies, "breakdown of financials by business line" was the most frequently mentioned item by analysts (80%) (see Figure 5.1).

Analysts were equally divided on the best time for a company to schedule a conference call. Thirty-three percent said, "before market

Table 5.1
Mean Averages: Summary of Evaluations

Communication Variables	All Respondents	Buy-Side Analysts	Sell-Side Analysts	Portfolio Managers	Other
Conference Calls - Value	4.36*	4.59	4.42	4.09	3.85
- Quality	4.17**	4.21	4.42	4.14	3.98
- Timeliness	4.43**	4.55	4.42	4.40	4.00
- Specificity	3.76**	3.83	3.92	3.82	3.41
Internet - - Value	3.57*	3.59	3.67	3.76	3.30
- Quality	3.72**	3.71	3.87	3.82	3.61
- Timeliness	3.32**	3.30	2.95	3.54	3.29
- Specificity	3.26**	3.32	3.13	3.31	3.08
E-mail- -Value	3.37*	3.47	3.13	3.24	3.23

*Using a 6-point scale, where 6 equals extremely valuable and 1 equals not at all valuable.
**Using a 6-point scale, where 6 equals outstanding and 1 equals poor.

opens"; 34 percent said, "during market hours"; and 33 percent said, "after market closes." Eighty-five percent of respondents said that the optimum length of formal remarks during conference calls was thirty minutes or less. Eighty-six percent said that the question and answer period should also be limited to thirty minutes or less.

Analysts reported a clear preference for notification of a conference call by e-mail (46%) or fax (39%). These analyst preferences contrast with the actual methods used by companies to publicize conference calls to individual investors and media: e-mail, 6 percent (for investors) and 4 percent (for media); fax, 71 percent (for both investors and

Figure 5.1
Additional Information Desired from Company Management during Conference Calls

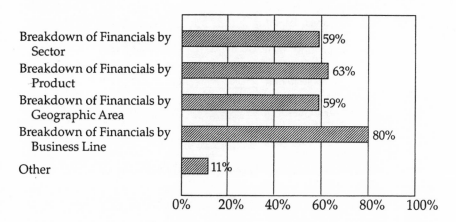

media). The majority of analysts (63%) included in the AIMR study said they would prefer no media participation in conference calls. Companies were even more restrictive. Among companies that hold conference calls, only 14 percent invited the media to participate, while only 12 percent allowed the media to participate in the question and answer segment of conference calls.[6]

Use of the Internet

The majority of analysts (66%) reported that "almost all" of the companies they followed have a corporate Web site, while the remainder (34%) said that "some" of the companies followed had a corporate Web site. This compares with 86 percent of companies in the NIRI study that have Web sites (as of February 1998). Of those companies with a corporate Web site, 44 percent of analysts said that "almost all" of these companies had an investor relations section, while 55 percent reported that "some" of the companies they followed had an IR section. In the NIRI survey, 86 percent of companies said that they sponsored an IR section on their Web sites.[7]

Annual reports (76%), quarterly earnings (72%), and other press releases (72%) are the most frequent types of information that companies provide on their Web sites, according to analysts in the AIMR study. Quarterly reports (65%), fact sheets/corporate profiles (62%), and SEC filings (60%) are also frequently provided on company Web sites, according to analysts (see Figure 5.2). Although the percentages

Figure 5.2
Types of Information That Companies Followed Provide on Their Web Sites

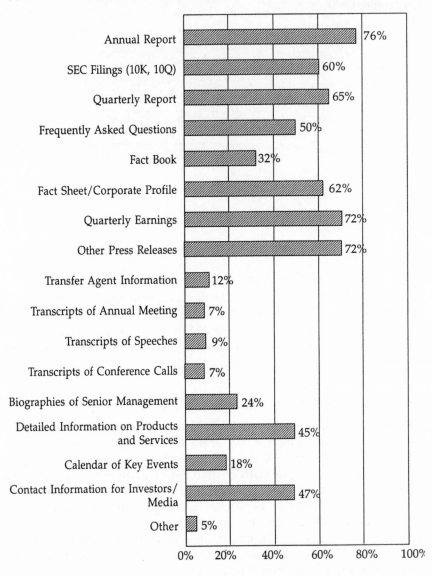

varied somewhat, these six types of information were among the most frequent items made available on corporate Web sites, according to IR officers in the NIRI study.[8]

As a source of strategic and financial information, 52 percent of analysts said the Internet was "somewhat valuable," 25 percent reported it was "very valuable," while 23 percent rated the Internet as "not valuable." On a 6-point scale, where 6 equals "extremely valuable" and 1 equals "not at all valuable," the mean average rating for all respondents was 3.57, as compared with 4.36 for conference calls. Breaking down mean average ratings by respondent position gives these results: buy-side analysts equals 3.59, sell-side analysts equals 3.67, portfolio managers equals 3.76, and other equals 3.30 (see Table 5.1).

When asked to rate their satisfaction with the overall usage of their company's Web sites, IR executive responses were remarkably similar to those of analysts. Fifty-two percent said the usage of their Web site to communicate with the investment community was "somewhat valuable"; 21 percent said it was "very valuable"; and 23 percent rated the use of the Internet as "not valuable."[9]

In the AIMR survey, 23 percent of the analysts rated the quality of strategic and financial information provided on a company Web site as "good" or "outstanding" (compared with 35% for conference calls). Only 21 percent evaluated the timeliness of information as "good" or "outstanding" (compared with a 53% rating for timeliness of conference calls). Fifteen percent of respondents rated the specificity of information provided on the Internet as "good" or "outstanding" (compared with a 20% rating for conference calls) (see Table 5.1).

While two-thirds of analysts reported that "almost all" of the strategic and financial information provided on the Internet was generally available from other sources, virtually the same number (65%) said that the availability of a company Web site "makes it easier to provide an accurate analysis of a company." Nevertheless, only 11 percent of respondents in the AIMR study reported logging on to their companies' Web sites hourly or daily, 24 percent said they logged on weekly, 41 percent logged on monthly, while 24 percent logged on quarterly. These findings contrast sharply with the results of a survey conducted by Straightline International in 1996. The Straightline study reported that 70 percent of analysts and money managers logged on at least once a week and 17 percent logged on daily.[10]

E-Mail

In the AIMR survey, 84 percent of analysts reported that some or almost all of the companies they followed use e-mail to communicate with the investment community. These findings are consistent with the results of the NIRI study that found that 63 percent of their member companies use e-mail to communicate with the investment community.[11]

As a source of strategic and financial information, analysts in the AIMR study rated e-mail as the least valuable of the major technologies surveyed. Fifty percent rated e-mail as "somewhat valuable," 22 percent as "very valuable," and 28 percent as "not valuable." On a 6-point scale where 6 equals "extremely valuable" and 1 equals "not at all valuable," the mean average rating for all respondents was 3.37, as compared with 3.57 for the Internet and 4.36 for conference calls. Breaking down mean average ratings by respondent position yields these results: buy-side analysts equals 3.47, sell-side analysts equals 3.13, portfolio managers equals 3.24, and other equals 3.23 (see Table 5.1).

Satisfaction of NIRI members with the usage of e-mail in their IR programs was similar to that of analysts in the AIMR survey. Forty-five percent of IR executives said that e-mail was "somewhat valuable," 22 percent said that it was "very valuable," while 32 percent reported that e-mail was "not valuable."[12]

Evaluation of Technology Use by Company Size

Analysts reported that those companies that made excellent use of technology in providing strategic and financial information tended to have larger market capitalization (cap.) companies ($1.5 billion or larger). Sixty-one percent of these "excellent technology usage" companies were large cap. corporations. When asked to identify the factors that made these companies effective in their use of technology, 72 percent of analysts said, "quality of information," 71 percent reported "timeliness of information," and 61 percent said "completeness of information" (see Figure 5.3).

Of those companies identified by analysts as not very effective in their use of technology, 14 percent had less than $100 million in market capitalization; 26 percent had $100 to $499 million; 21 percent had $.5 to $1.5 billion, and 39 percent had $1.5 billion or more. According to analysts, reasons for ineffectiveness were "doesn't use technology" (54%), "lack of information" (53%), "lack of timely information" (42%), and "incomplete information" (42%) (see Figure 5.4).

ANALYSIS AND DISCUSSION

Neither investor relations executives nor analysts appear to be overly enthusiastic with the current usage of financial communications technology. Analysts rate conference calls as superior to the Internet or e-mail as a source of strategic and financial information. Commenting on the results of the AIMR survey, Tom Bowman, president and CEO of AIMR, observed,

The value, quality, timeliness and specificity of strategic and financial information provided in conference calls is considered superior to that provided on the Internet or through e-mail. This seems to indicate that direct access to the CFO, CEO and investor relations officer remains an important factor when

Figure 5.3
Market Capitalization of Companies That Make Excellent Use of Technology in Providing Strategic and Financial Information

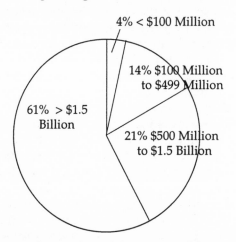

Note: Thirty-two percent of respondents did not answer this question.

Figure 5.4
Market Capitalization of Companies That Are Not Very Effective in Their Use of Technology in Providing Strategic and Financial Information

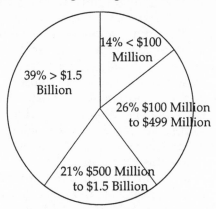

Note: Forty percent of respondents did not answer this question.

trying to evaluate the potential of a company and its stock price. AIMR Senior VP Ray DeAngelo noted that access to top company officials is the clear reason why conference calls are preferred by analysts. But DeAngelo wondered if Internet communication won't close the gap at some point in the future. "The Internet, in terms of familiarity of technology, is where conference calls were 10 to 15 years ago."[13]

Given the lack of high-quality, timely, specific information on the Internet, the availability of information from other sources, and the fact that many analysts apparently don't have a need to follow the daily or weekly vagaries of the companies they follow, it probably is not surprising that the majority of analysts log on to their companies' Web sites so infrequently. In fact, "Lou Thompson, President of the National Investor Relations Institute, said he was 'encouraged' by the use of the Internet by analysts [as reported in the AIMR study], and was actually surprised that it was that high given all the sources of information available to analysts."[14]

While companies are investing significant corporate resources in new communications technologies, the full potential of these technologies remains to be achieved. As the NIRI survey has revealed, IR executives themselves are not particularly satisfied with the usage of their Web sites or e-mail, and the findings of the AIMR study are not likely to boost corporate satisfaction levels. While not particularly positive, constructive feedback from analysts—prime users of strategic and financial information—can be of value to companies. Also, lessons from successful, more mature technologies, such as conference calls, can be instructive when applied to new technologies such as the Internet. "Financial Relations Board president Theodore Pincus, whose firm is the largest investor relations specialist in the country, believes that live video conferencing will be the next major advance in the use of the Internet. His company is currently beta-testing a software program called Contigo that will enable companies to communicate directly via the Internet with analysts around the country and around the world."[15]

What obstacles do companies face as they seek to achieve a more effective utilization of new technology? One barrier appears to be a threat of securities litigation. Despite recent reforms, "Companies are clearly concerned that any additional information they provide online is covered by the same laws that cover written communication with shareholders and [that] any forward-looking statement could leave them open to a lawsuit if earnings fail to meet expectations."[16] As reported in Chapter 4, this litigation appears to have had a serious dampening effect on the willingness of U.S. companies to release future-oriented corporate statements. To minimize this threat, "One thing companies could be doing is making available the most current estimates of analysts," says Carl Thompson, whose firm was one of the first to take advantage of the Internet. "[Companies] could also be posting transcripts from conference calls they hold with analysts, so that individual investors get access to the conversations that companies have with money managers on Wall Street."[17]

Another factor is cost. According to Tom Bowman, AIMR president,

The expenses of upgrading the Investor Relations portion of the corporate web site may be high, but companies should deem the benefits of providing information to the financial community sufficient to offset the costs. As seen in our survey, however, corporations have not yet done this as analysts are disappointed by the quality, timeliness and specificity of financial information provided on the Internet. . . . Ray DeAngelo, Senior VP at AIMR, said the findings on Internet usage are . . . a bit of a chicken-and-egg question. Analysts might log on to a corporate web site only a few times because they're not getting updated information, but companies won't update information if analysts aren't logging on.[18]

The Internet, however powerful its potential, is still basically a tool— a medium—to transmit messages to the investment community. As important as the medium is in financial communications, the message is equally significant. Feedback obtained from analysts and portfolio managers in the AIMR survey reaffirms the importance of message content. Although the basic thrust of this feedback may have a familiar ring to it, it is just as valid today as it was a decade ago. Analysts hate surprises. Regardless of the medium or technology employed, they want timely, specific, quality information and they want it in bad times as well as good.

Companies that have taken these lessons to heart are rewarded in a variety of ways, as reported in Chapters 2 and 3. Strategic credibility is not necessarily awarded to those companies with the largest and most sophisticated arsenal of communications technology. It is bestowed on those firms that use this technology to deliver consistent, candid, credible messages to the investment community. In Part II of this book, we will meet a number of these companies.

NOTES

1. "Net Worth," *Reputation Management* 3 (November/December 1997): 26.
2. Ibid.
3. Ibid.
4. Rivel Research Group, "Utilizing Technology in the Practice of Investor Relations," Second Measurement, April 1998 (a study conducted for the National Investor Relations Institute among Senior Investor Relations Executives at NIRI Companies by Rivel Research Group), 5.
5. Ibid., 7.
6. Ibid., 12.
7. Ibid., 8.
8. Ibid., 16.
9. Ibid., 17.
10. "Net Worth," 27.
11. Rivel Research Group, "Utilizing Technology," 18.

12. Ibid., 19.

13. "Analysts Like Conference Calls but Websites Are Not Up to Snuff," *Investor Relations Business*, 1 March 1999, 14.

14. Ibid.

15. "Net Worth," 28.

16. Ibid.

17. Ibid.

18. "Analysts Like Conference Calls," 14.

PART II

CASES IN GLOBAL STRATEGIC AND FINANCIAL COMMUNICATIONS: UNITED STATES, EUROPE, AND JAPAN

6

AT&T: Communication in the Midst of Change

Connie Weaver

Communications is the leading growth industry of the global economy, growing three to four times as fast as the world's gross national product. By all accounts this growth will continue into the foreseeable future. The most advanced and competitive communications market is in the United States, where the industry is in the midst of a technological revolution. Emerging technology is fast eliminating the barriers that now separate local, long distance, Internet, entertainment, and wireless services. AT&T is a leading contestant in this industry transformation toward what it calls an "any-distance" marketplace. Once primarily a domestic long-distance voice business, AT&T is rapidly becoming a global broadband communications company that can provide any application, any service, any place in the world with one connection.

To get to this brave new world, the corporation has acquired major assets and set up joint ventures with formidable industry partners. Acquisitions have included TCG, a leading provider of local business services; TCI, formerly the country's second largest cable company; IBM's Global Networking business; and Vanguard, a cellular business. AT&T also set up multibillion-dollar joint ventures with major players like BT and Time Warner, and still others with TCI affiliates (see Table 6.1 for a summary of recent acquisitions and joint ventures).

Table 6.1
Recent Major AT&T Acquisitions and Joint Ventures

Date	Company	Value
January 1998	**TCG** – local business services	$11.0 billion
June 1998	**TCI** – cable, video, data and telephony services	$48.0 billion
December 1998	**IBM Global Network** – global data services	$ 5.0 billion
October 1998	**Vanguard** – wireless services	$ 1.5 billion
July 1998	**BT** (Joint venture) – global communications services	Not applicable
April 1999	**MediaOne** – cable, video, data and telephony services	$62 billion
Pending	**Time Warner** (Joint venture) – cable telephony services	Not applicable

GROWING AND ON THE OFFENSIVE

It is a tremendous change for the company. The AT&T of today and tomorrow is radically different from the AT&T of yesterday. We are in the midst of redefining the industry and ourselves and taking advantage of unprecedented growth opportunities. We are moving from narrow band to broadband, from circuit switched to packet switched, from product focused to customer and market focused, and from a commodity environment to a differentiated environment where our services add value that cannot easily be replicated, are affordable, and make a world of difference in people's lives.

A glimpse of that "difference" is already evident in wireless calling. With simplified pricing and long battery life, wireless phones are increasingly becoming universal phones. AT&T's Digital One Rate does that and more for a flat fee, with no roaming charges for calls anywhere in the United States. Launched in 1998, the service has been selling off the shelf ever since. Another example is the technology AT&T is testing with cable television. It transforms the set-top box on the TV into a communications device and information-management tool. When deployed, this box will enable customers to add phone lines, forward calls, retrieve messages, and access the Internet. All this in addition to doing what it has hitherto done: provide entertainment.

An industry giant that was on the defensive less than two years ago, AT&T has clearly gone on the offensive. It is not trying to hold on to market share anymore. It is aggressively going after it. Mike Armstrong, who was elected chairman and CEO in November 1997, is leading the company in this new proactive approach. A hands-on, dynamic business leader, Armstrong came to AT&T from Hughes Electronics, where he had been chairman and CEO for six years, transforming it from a company focused mainly on defense to a powerful competitor in the commercial electronics, space, and telecommunications industries. Prior to Hughes, he spent three decades at IBM, where he rose through the ranks to become senior vice president and chairman of the board of IBM World Trade Corporation.

These are truly exciting times, more exciting than any in the company's history. We are redefining the industry and we are deploying a new generation of technology. In less than two years we have gone from a $50-billion company to almost a $200-billion company in terms of market capitalization.

COMMUNICATING WITH INVESTORS

Through this rapid transition to any-distance communications, AT&T had to make sure that the investing community was kept abreast of developments, understood the reasoning behind them, and was generally on board. In time of great change, it is critical to keep investors informed about the reasons for these moves. Communicating openly, fully, and quickly is of utmost importance. It is what determines the level of confidence these constituents have in you. It is what determines your credibility.

The IR role is more than one-way communication from the company to Wall Street. A good IR organization is a conduit for two-way communication. It provides information about the company to the marketplace and it brings information back to the company's senior management so the leadership team understands how the company is perceived. The objective is to make sure that perception and reality are in sync (see Figure 6.1, describing the IR organization at AT&T).

This view of open, honest two-way communication began to pay off early in the transition to an any-distance communications business. When shareowners were asked to approve the merger with TCI in early 1999, for example, some 75 percent of eligible shareowners participated in the vote, a historic high. Moreover, 99 percent of those who voted supported the merger, another historic high. I don't believe we could have had these election results without a strong, effective communications effort. Another indicator may be the stock price.

Figure 6.1
Organization of Investor Relations at AT&T

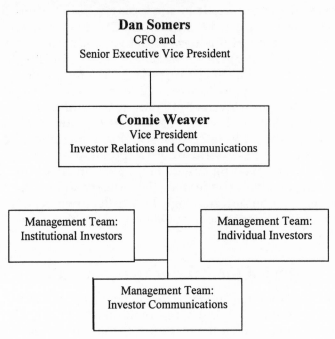

It has almost tripled in less than two years, going from $32 in 1997 to over $80 before it was split in the first quarter of 1999.

GROWING THE BUSINESS

To get to any-distance services and increase shareholder value, AT&T is focusing on five growth markets: local, online services, network consulting and outsourcing, wireless, and international. The company's acquisitions and joint ventures are part of a facilities-based strategy designed to support this market focus. It ends the resale approach to market that dominated the industry since divestiture of the Bell system in 1984. The resale approach required the competitive segment of the industry, AT&T and the other long-distance carriers, to resell the services of the monopoly sector, the regional Bell operating companies (RBOCs) in the United States and the public telephone services overseas. The following list summarizes AT&T's major competitors:

- MCI Worldcom
- Sprint
- Regional Bell Operating Companies (SBC, Bell Atlantic)
- Deutsche Telekom (pending merger with Telecom Italia)
- France telecom
- NTT

The facilities-based strategy gives AT&T three distinct advantages over resale:

- Marketplace access, which is currently monopolized by the regional operating companies.
- Control of architecture, the specifications, interfaces, protocols, standards, and platforms necessary to provide global seamless services.
- Control of costs, which can only be achieved by owning facilities end to end.

MANAGING THE RELATIONSHIP WITH SHAREOWNERS

Change in strategy. Change in technology. Change in market terrain and opportunities. It is a challenge to communicate and explicate so much change to shareowners who are used to a steadier pace. AT&T's stock is among the most widely held in the United States. The diversity of owners ranges from individuals with a handful of shares to major institutions who may own millions of shares.

AT&T has 3.3 million individual shareowners. They hold some 45 percent of the stock. Institutional investors hold the remaining 55 percent. We segment our shareowners into broad categories and then try to serve their respective informational needs, which are very different. Individual investors, for example, range from the very sophisticated, who trade regularly, to people who've held the stock for a long time and may be very unsophisticated. On the institutional side, there are a number of groupings. One consists of analysts. They do not buy or sell stocks; they advise others and command large channels of communications for their views. Understanding their objectives, what they do, and how they go about differentiating themselves to their audiences, the investors, is very important.

Then there are the investors themselves: large and small institutions and portfolio managers. Highly sophisticated, this group is animated by a range of factors ("styles") that an IR program must take into account. When you walk into a brokerage house, there are multiple styles and some people will own your stock at different points in time. You have to know who they are, and know as much about what their ownership appetite is as you can. It is no different than segmenting a market, where different customers have different sets of needs. Investors' needs are informational: 50 percent for financial data and 50 percent for qualitative information. Do you have a strategy? Do you have a strong management team? Can you execute the strategy? How innovative are you? What kind of talent do you attract? (See Table 6.2 for a summary breakdown of AT&T shareholders.)

A STRATEGIC COMMUNICATIONS VEHICLE

Companies like AT&T use several vehicles to communicate with these audiences: press releases, conference calls to announce earnings, major deals (a la TCI or Time Warner), quarterly reports, and product launches. Not surprisingly, the Web is fast emerging as a strategic vehicle. The reason is that it is fast, and it provides direct access to information a la carte to all audiences. Unlike information provided via a press release, information on the Web is not mediated by a third party—a reporter. It goes nonstop and without comment from the company to the investor. The Web is the next best thing to face-to-face communication. It is efficient, a cost saver, and convenient both for investors and the company. For individual investors it means easy access to personal accounts and to a host of other valuable information. With the changes in the company over the last couple of years, especially the Lucent and NCR spin-offs, calculating your taxes can be a nightmare because the stock has gone through so many shifts. We get many calls from individual investors for old prices and old dividend records for their IRS filings. We can now refer callers to our Web site, which saves us a significant amount of time and money.

On the institutional side, the Web's effectiveness for AT&T is suggested by the virtual disappearance of "complaining calls." Before our IR site went up, after every announcement we used to be bombarded by calls from analysts and investors who did not receive the release: Their fax line was down, their equipment was busy, or there were transmission delays. Now that they have access to our site, those calls have virtually disappeared. It is rare these days for us to get that kind of a call.

The Internet is also a dynamic vehicle. Information can readily be updated, corrected, or enriched with additional information. Good sites are user friendly, affording easy, equal access when it is wanted. Unlike hard-copy reports that take time to produce and distribute, Web distribution is virtually instantaneous. The Web also enables us to release more information to the investing community today than we have ever done before. The market demands it and now we have the vehicle to facilitate that demand.

Table 6.2
Summary Breakdown of AT&T Shareholders

Shareholder & Influencers	Profile/Perspectives
Individual Investor	3.3 million individual shareowners -- 58% own less than 100 shares -- 33% reinvest dividends -- $100 million invested per quarter
Institutional: Sell-Side	Provide investment advice and analysis to the buy-side and write research reports. Sell-side includes: -- Research analysts -- Institutional sales people -- Retail brokers -- Traders
Institutional: Buy-Side	*Passively managed:* investment choices predetermined by formula rather than made at the discretion of managers. Example: index funds or funds that own the top 10 dividend yielding stocks on the Dow. *Actively managed:* investment choices made according to decision-making processes specific to each firm and vary by fund. Decisions made by portfolio managers or committees of managers who rely on a variety of sources. Internal research analysts and sell-side analysts are key sources.
Other: International owners	While foreign ownership data are not precise since foreign firms do not have the same filing requirements as US firms, we know that about 6% of our total shares outstanding are held internationally. A majority of these are held in Europe: 30% in the UK, 27% in Switzerland and 18% in Germany.

THE MAKINGS OF AN EFFECTIVE TOOL

These advantages of the Web do not come easily. Stephanie Roberts, vice president of production services at Elemental Interactive Design and Development, Atlanta, comments, "Establishing and maintaining a site is time consuming. It requires a dedicated staff and money. IR sites are a relatively new phenomenon for companies. So it's important to set proper expectation levels for the amount of time and money it takes to build and maintain a Web site. Even when companies are willing to put a lot of effort in creating an IR site, they often don't fund it adequately and don't put in place the internal processes to maintain the content on that site."

For IR Web sites to be effective, Roberts recommends that they be managed and maintained by a company's IR organization, the people who know and interact with the audience for that site, and not by a corporate communications or marketing group, although feedback and ideas from these groups could be valuable. The look, the feel, and the content of the site should reflect the informational needs and sensibilities of investors. The IR site may need to be different from the corporate Web site—to better support the specific target audiences.

Moreover, the IR site should take into account the various groups being addressed. The kind of information an analyst is interested in may be different from the information the individual investor is looking for. Roberts's research is very telling on this. "Analysts want direct, quick access to such information as SEC filings, press releases, quarterly earnings, overviews or fact sheets about the company and industry, and conference call information. By contrast, individual investors are more concerned with new product and service information, how the company stacks up against the competition and information about the stock."

These different interests are reflected in the different languages to which the two respond. According to Roberts, "Analysts, when they visit an IR site, look for the words 'press release.' Individual shareholders are more familiar with the word 'news.' 'Press release' doesn't seem to mean a whole lot to them. It's not the hook they follow on the information trail."

ASSESSING EFFECTIVENESS

To gauge the effectiveness of an existing site on the intended audience and gain input on how to make it more so, the author recommends the use of usability studies, one for each intended audience. These studies try to answer some basic questions. How easy is this site to use? Is the presentation of information effective? Is it organized in a way that makes it easily accessible?

AT&T underwent a usability study in late 1998 to help guide a pending site redesign. The research focused on the behaviors and preferences of a handful of target users. In general, these are not especially elaborate studies. Each session takes two to three hours and requires only a room with a computer hooked to the IR Web site, a user (analyst or individual shareholder), and a facilitator who is an objective observer not connected to the IR organization. The two follow a series of scenarios appropriate for that user. The facilitator assesses how quickly and efficiently the user is able to access information. The user is encouraged to think out loud so that the facilitator can follow his or her thought processes.

The challenge in such a study is to identify the right representative of the intended audience. "For the AT&T study, New York City proved to be a better source for an AT&T analyst than Atlanta," says Roberts. Findings from AT&T's usability study influenced their 1999 redesign of information architecture (natural groupings of topics, etc.) and the graphical user interface (colors, placement/shape of buttons, etc.). The process is ongoing, though, and subsequent site updates will most likely include new studies in the up-front stages.

Web-based communication does not replace other communications vehicles. It complements them. And one way to increase traffic to the site is to promote it in the other vehicles. Audiences should be directed to the Web for more information, for updates, and for information about related issues. Every communication from us (IR organization) always refers the audience to the Web. We include the company's URL on our dividend checks.

LEVERAGING THE MEDIUM

Another way to increase traffic is to offer something extra to visitors that would not be feasible in a print publication or other vehicles, thus using the site as a competitive tool. Roberts points to three examples: IBM, Microsoft, and AT&T.

IBM has a guide to understanding financials, complete with a glossary of terms. That's a very powerful tool, for it educates shareholders on how to read a financial statement.

Microsoft leverages the power of the medium. It provides live online conference calls to site visitors, broadening audience access to information previously limited to large institutional holders, analysts and the financial press.

AT&T has the most content of any IR site I've seen. It's by far the leader. What I like the most is the easy access it provides analysts to information of value to them. The subtext reads: "We know who you are, we know what your information needs are and here is quick access to it."

A helpful, appealing site builds confidence in the company. It's subliminal, but it's there. "I invest in this company for shareowner value," say investors. And when they go to that site they can sense that value.

RISKS

The risks associated with Web-based communications are relatively few. Information provided online must follow the same basic rules of disclosure as information provided via hard copy and is generally covered by the same laws that cover all other written communication with shareholders. You have to be mindful of anything you disclose, regardless of medium. On the technical side, the server may go down. But that is less likely to happen if adequate resources and expertise are dedicated up front. And with the current level of available technology, it should not be a frequent occurrence. The greatest risk is in poor execution: designing a site that is not friendly, does not contain the information visitors need and want, and is more glitter than substance. Investors should have their confidence in the company reinforced: aesthetically, substantively, and subliminally. "Companies must realize that sites are 'alive,'" adds Roberts. They require constant nurturing. "You can't put up a site and assume that you're done, that you've fulfilled the needs of your audience. Managing a site is a process of continuous refinement."

Web-based communication with the investing community will increase exponentially, especially after AT&T and others deploy broadband channels. Individual investors will have fast, state-of-the-art access to IR sites. The Web is quickly becoming a transactional medium as well, not only providing investors with the information they need to make decisions, but also the ability to act on them. The communication challenge will not be the medium. It will be the message: consistently open and honest communication that informs investors in good—and not so good—times.

7

Investor Relations at Schering-Plough Corporation: When Less Is More

Geraldine U. Foster
and Stephen K. Galpin, Jr.

Over the past decade the investor relations program at Schering-Plough has aspired above all else to create, promote, and sustain relationships with Schering-Plough's financial constituents that demonstrate the commitment of senior management to fair and complete disclosure. The company believes creating and maintaining a world-class investor relations program is not difficult, but it does require a rigorous adherence to what Schering-Plough calls the "Four Cs of Investor Relations": *compliance* with all federal, exchange, and moral requirements of disclosure; *credibility* with both the external financial community and internal management; *commitment* of that management to the principles and practices of investor relations; and last, but perhaps most important, *consistency* in everything that is said and done (see Figure 7.1).

The company's investor relations team also seeks to be as creative in communicating as the market (and management!) can bear, using a number of innovative publications, forms of meetings, and other sometimes unusual ways to communicate Schering-Plough's performance and strategic direction. Perhaps one of the most meaningful compliments that has ever been paid to the program was one analyst's characterization of it as "simple but elegant." Other more formal honors bestowed on the program and its practitioners include top ranking for the health-care category by the Corporate Information Committee (CIC) of the Association for Investment Research and Management for six consecutive years. In its 1993–1994 report, the CIC noted, "Schering-Plough has long been an industry leader in providing quality information to the financial community. For the past several years, it has made senior managers available to investment professionals for

Figure 7.1
Four "Cs" of IR

- ## Compliance

- ## Credibility

- ## Commitment

- ## Consistency

open and frank discussions at annual meetings. The company has also been an innovator in disclosing detailed quarterly sales data by major product lines."

Under the leadership of Richard Jay Kogan, the present chairman and chief executive officer; Raul E. Cesan, president and chief operating officer; and Hugh A. D'Andrade, vice chairman and chief administrative officer (to whom the investor relations position reports), Schering-Plough is thriving. With more than $8 billion in sales reported in 1998, the company's blockbuster product, the nonsedating antihistamine Claritin, racked up sales of $2.3 billion in 1998. Schering-Plough currently enjoys a market value among the top thirty in the *Fortune* 500, and 1998 marked its thirteenth consecutive year of double-digit growth in earnings per share. From 1986 through 1998 the company declared fifteen dividend increases and five two-for-one stock splits and has completed ten share repurchase programs. These activities further underscore the proposition that this is a company that seeks to enhance shareholder value (see Figure 7.2).

Most important, this is a company that can be accurately described as one that values its investors, treats them as partners in Schering-Plough's success, and strives to keep them informed and to be responsive to their needs. How does Schering-Plough's IR staff know what

Figure 7.2
SGP Rewards Shareholders

13th	Consecutive Year of Double-Digit EPS Growth
15	Dividend Increases Since 1986
5	Two-for-One Stock Splits Since 1987
34.6%	Ten-Year Compound Annual Rate of Return *

*As of December 31, 1998.

investors want? They ask! Written evaluations after major meetings, one-on-one conversations, and informal telephone surveys provide valuable insight into what is important to investors and how to provide that information in useful and accessible formats. This is why Schering-Plough's investor relations program is thriving.

THE ORIGINS OF SCHERING-PLOUGH

Schering-Plough's roots are in Europe and can be traced back to the mid-1800s, when a Berlin-based company founded by Dr. Ernest Schering established a U.S. distribution branch. The company was in operation until it was nationalized during World War I. Schering reestablished U.S. operations in the 1920s, incorporating in New York City in 1928. Five years later the company crossed the Hudson River to set up operations in East Orange, New Jersey. Meanwhile, the Plough Chemical Company was formed in Memphis, Tennessee, in 1908 by a young entrepreneur named Abe Plough. The firm made a name for itself selling the leading brand of children's aspirin, St. Joseph's.

Schering Corp. was again nationalized by the U.S. government during World War II. Following the war, the company remained under government control until 1952, when a group of investors led by Merrill Lynch purchased Schering Corp. and subsequently sold shares to the public.

In 1971 Schering Corporation and Plough, Inc. merged to become Schering-Plough Corporation (NYSE: SGP). The combined product lines of the new company included prescription and over-the-counter pharmaceuticals, veterinary products, cosmetics, proprietary drugs and toiletries, home repair products, and even radio stations. In 1971 sales totaled $450 million, positioning Schering-Plough as one of the top pharmaceutical companies in the United States. Throughout that decade, drug sales were led by the popular antibiotic Garamycin. The company made further inroads into anti-infective markets with the introduction of the broad-spectrum antifungal Lotrimin and into the important respiratory sector with Vanceril, an asthma medication, which debuted in 1976.

By 1975 Schering-Plough's professional roster included 1,200 scientists and technicians, more than double the number in the previous decade. As the 1970s drew to a close, the company launched a major strategic initiative into the emerging area of biotechnology, purchasing a minority equity interest in Biogen, Inc. in 1979. In January 1980 Biogen announced it had produced the human leukocyte alpha interferon through genetic engineering. Schering-Plough, which had exclusive worldwide marketing rights to Biogen's alpha-2 interferon, took the lead in investigating potential therapeutic uses of the substance. Clinical studies on antiviral and anticancer applications were pursued, and the foundations were set for a full in-house research and development capability in biotechnology.

SGP MANAGEMENT AND ITS STRATEGIC VISION

Schering-Plough began the 1980s with a new, visionary management team headed by Robert P. Luciano, who left Ciba-Geigy to join the company in 1978, subsequently bringing in two colleagues, Richard Jay Kogan and Hugh A. D'Andrade. Luciano became president and chief operating officer in 1980, chief executive officer in 1982, and added the title of chairman in 1984. Kogan assumed the position of president and chief operating officer in 1986, and D'Andrade was named executive vice president, administration. This management team created the strategic vision that would carry the company not just through the next decade, but into the millennium.

By the end of the 1980s the Luciano management team had established a bold blueprint for growth. It included ongoing substantial investment in research and development in select therapeutic areas; capital investment in state-of-the-art facilities; divestiture of businesses that did not fit the strategic focus; active pursuit of growth through acquisitions, joint ventures, and product and technology licensing agreements; and a continued emphasis on operating efficiency. It thus became clear in short order that it would be the job of the investor relations department not only to communicate these strategies to the Wall Street community, but also to convince followers that these were strategies for success.

THE STATE OF IR IN 1990

When she arrived in February 1988 as the vice president for investor relations, Geraldine U. Foster found Schering-Plough's investor relations program to be widely regarded as one of the best in the industry. Only a few of Schering-Plough's peer companies had dedicated investor relations officers, let alone programs. Top management's appointment of an IR executive who reported directly to the executive office was ahead of its time.

Still, the program at Schering-Plough was largely reactive and focused on a handful of sell-side analysts. If an analyst telephoned, he or she was called back. A cadre of executives traveled to Europe once a year, giving speeches at major financial centers. Press releases were mailed out and analyst reports were read and circulated. An on-site, half-day analysts meeting was organized annually at Schering-Plough's manufacturing facility in New Jersey, at which management and leading research scientists gave detailed presentations. There was little additional contact with investors other than at the one health-care conference the company attended annually.

In short, the investor relations program had all the *markings* of a modern program, but none of the *makings* of a superior one. It was not a marketing program; it was basically a customer-service function. However, the essential building blocks to create a superior marketing-oriented IR program were present: supportive management; a liberal, even radical corporate structure that placed the IR function in a position of influence; and an investor relations officer with a strong marketing background.

Indeed, from the moment Gerry Foster arrived on the scene, she had the full and unqualified support of then-CEO Robert P. Luciano, a precedent continued through to today by his successor Richard Jay Kogan. These executives established an open-door policy that not only allowed (and continues to encourage) investors to come in for face-to-face meetings, but also makes the executive office truly part of the process of investing in Schering-Plough. This was an utterly radical notion in the early 1990s, a time when investor relations in the pharmaceutical industry was often relegated to the treasury function.

At Schering-Plough, moreover, corporate communications today is completely integrated with investor relations. IR takes the lead in shaping the corporation's messages, supported and complemented by the corporate communications function. Specialized expertise in the corporate communications department in investor communications, media relations, and internal communications is relied upon by both departments. There are no turf wars over financial press releases, and the hallmarks of both the corporate communications and investor relations programs are efficiency and consistency within each function and across departmental lines.

It is interesting to note that when Gerry Foster joined Schering-Plough she and an executive secretary were the entire staff. She added one professional position shortly thereafter, and a second in 1996. Investor relations and corporate communications were combined into one department in 1994, when Ms. Foster was named senior vice president of investor relations and corporate communications. Today, the combined professional staff is only eleven people, many of whom have been with the company more than ten years and have a thorough knowledge of its operations and a strong commitment to communicating its strategic messages. Since 1994 the staff has worked as a single unit to develop and communicate a consistent, credible message to Schering-Plough's shareholders (see Figure 7.3 for the organization of investor relations and corporate communications at Schering-Plough).

The unofficial motto of the entire financial communications program is "less is more." This means that the company continually aims to give its investor exactly what they want and need. Further, the marketing orientation of the present program is entirely congruous with the overall marketing outlook of the company. The "less is more" philosophy also applies to the investor relations function: Gerry Foster's IR team includes two professionals and two administrative people, and the overflow administrative work is handled by college interns.

Two simple diagrams illustrate how information flows at Schering-Plough. The flow for investor relations is basically a triangle that includes management, investor relations, and investors. Strategic information flows from management through investor relations to investors and then returns, in the form of feedback, from investors through investor relations to management (see Figure 7.4).

The flow of financial communications demonstrates the dynamics between investor relations, the media, and investors. Information flows from management to both investor relations and corporate communications. As appropriate, IR shares the information with investors and corporate communications passes it along to the press (and the general

Figure 7.3
Investor Relations and Corporate Communications

Senior Vice President
IR and Corporate Communications

Staff Vice President
Investor Relations

Staff Vice President
Corporate Communications

Investor Relations
(1 Person)

Writing and Research
(2 People)

Employee Communications
(2 People)

Media Relations
(5 People)

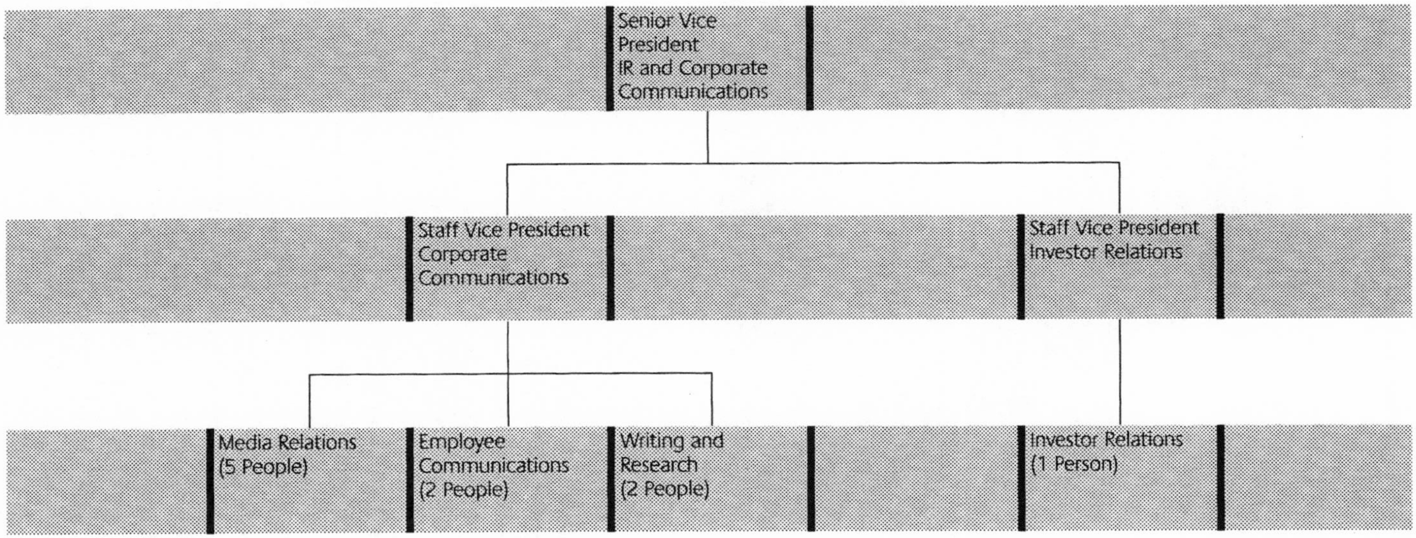

Figure 7.4
The Investor Relations Triangle

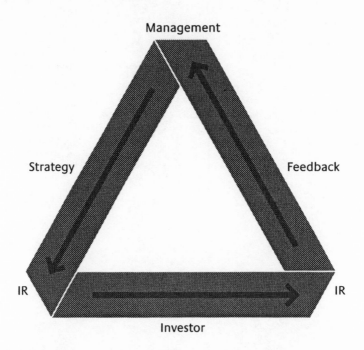

public) in the form of press releases. The media, in turn, often contact investors for comments when news about SGP breaks. Again, feedback, based on media coverage, questions from reporters, and investor comments, is routinely provided to management (see Figure 7.5).

It was CEO Luciano's vision that the company was on the upswing, and that SGP owed it to the shareholders to deliver a fully valued stock. He also believed that by delivering earnings consistently quarter after quarter, the market would recognize this and the stock would appreciate accordingly. Under Luciano's leadership, it became an overriding objective at Schering-Plough to become a consistent performer with a clear, steady message. Taking its cues from the product-marketing philosophies of the company, investor relations began to develop an efficient marketing profile, giving its customers—the investors—exactly what they needed without frills.

At Schering-Plough, internal financial communications are virtually as important as those to the external world. It was an early mission of the new investor relations team to establish a consciousness

Figure 7.5
Financial Communications

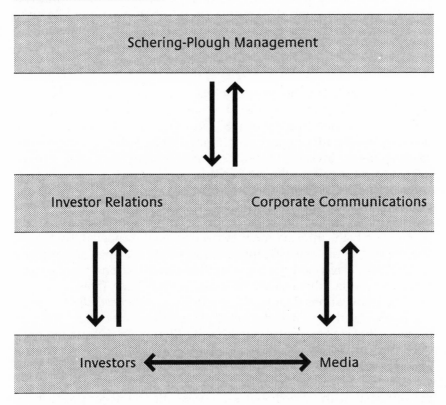

within the organization about the outside world's perception of Schering-Plough. Groups of managers were invited to attend formal presentations about the nature and purpose of investor relations, and a review of the investor relations program was presented to the board of directors. A white paper on the current state of investor relations was delivered to the Schering-Plough Operating Committee in 1995. (An updated adaptation of this paper was published in the professional journal *Investor Relations Quarterly*, Volume 1, Number 1, Summer 1997).

In 1996 a senior management communications program was launched to include the company's top 500 managers around the world in the investor relations program. This group, informally dubbed "The Fortunate 500," regularly receives the publications sent to the investment community. Information about the investor relations program is conveyed quarterly to all employees in *Schering-Plough World*, which is published by corporate communications. In addition, the larger employee community is kept informed of industry-related news and Wall Street's views through the company's intranet-distributed *Morning Highlights* and *The Closing Bell*, which is also delivered via e-mail.

LAYING THE FOUNDATIONS

In the early 1900s the company was in a phase of rebuilding and regeneration, having more or less bottomed out when its leading drug, Garamycin, went off-patent in 1980. Schering-Plough had just started on an upward path of positive earnings and had also undergone one stock split—an investor-friendly strategic activity that would be repeated four times over the next decade.

By the fall of 1989 the investor relations department at Schering-Plough had begun to roll out a number of highly innovative and widely praised publications, all aimed at putting into investors' and analysts' hands exactly the information they need when they need it. Each piece was created to fill a specific information need for a specific audience. A uniform design tied the look of all the publications together and readily identified them as an "SGP publication" (see Table 7.1).

Three publications debuted late in 1989: the *Financial Update, Investor Insights*, and the *Product Pipeline*. This triumvirate offers users all the news that is fit to print about Schering-Plough's performance, practices, and prospects. The *Financial Update* is an attractive package of materials broadly distributed to follow and amplify the company's quarterly earnings releases. It includes statements of consolidated income and the same data with ratios-to-sales analysis, sales by major product category, consolidated balance sheets, and statements of consolidated cash flows. Analysts especially praise the page that displays two-year quarterly data, which allows them to discern trends (see Table 7.2).

Investor Insights is published every other month. A single sheet of standard letter-size paper printed on both sides, it displays key dates, research insights, regulatory insights, insights from operating units, and investor relations items. *Investor Insights* concludes with the Final Word, a sometimes offbeat look at aspects of Schering-Plough's business. Final Words have included poetry, word-scramble and crossword puzzle contests, and reports about elementary school students using company products in science experiments. Contests feature prizes of Schering-Plough products or promotional material for the first ten or so people to fax back correct responses. The real value of the Final Word, however, is that it gives the investor relations department a good idea of who has been reading *Investor Insights*—and who has turned it over to read it through to the end (see Figure 7.6).

Table 7.1
SGP Investor Relations Publications

Year Begun	Publication	Description
Existing	Annual Report	
Existing	Investor Bulletin	Summary of major executive speeches to investors
1989	Financial Update	Quarterly financial information
1989	Investor Insights	Update on products, research and events at SGP
1989	Product Pipeline	Streamlined chart of all products in development
1992	Investor Financial Review	Comprehensive compendium of financial statistics and information
1996	Rx Deals	Overview of strategic licensing and marketing agreements
1997	Glossary	Definitions of product-related medical and research vocabulary
1998	SPIRAL (Schering-Plough Investor Relations Analysts Literature)	Spiral-bound compendium of important financial documents
1998	ADAM's RIB (A Day at Madison's Review in Brief)	Summary of ADAM meeting proceedings

ADDITIONAL PUBLICATIONS

Arguably the most critical of all publications prepared by Schering-Plough's investor relations department is the SGP *Product Pipeline*, which is updated and distributed about six times annually. In a simple four-page format, the *Product Pipeline* captures the essence of the company's future—compounds in various stages of clinical development—and lays it out for the investment community to see, clearly, simply, and accurately.

Other publications that have been added include the *Investor Financial Review*, which offers fact-book-type detailed information of com-

Table 7.2
Financial Update: Statements of Consolidated Income (Dollars in Millions, except EPS)

	1998							1997									1996
	1st Qtr $	2nd Qtr $	6 Mos $	3rd Qtr $	9 Mos $	4th Qtr $	Year $	1st Qtr $	2nd Qtr $	6 Mos $	3rd Qtr $	9 Mos $	4th Qtr $	Year $	4th Qtr vs. 4th Qtr	12 Mos vs. 12 Mos	Year $
Net Sales	1,908	2,124	4,032	1,986	6,018	2,059	8,077	1,568	1,720	3,288	1,709	4,997	1,781	6,778	16%	19%	5,656
Cost of Sales	380	423	803	394	1,197	404	1,601	289	330	619	326	945	363	1,308	11%	22%	1,078
Gross Margin	1,528	1,701	3,229	1,592	4,821	1,655	6,476	1,279	1,390	2,669	1,383	4,052	1,418	5,470	17%	18%	4,578
Total SG&A	712	828	1,540	762	2,302	839	3,141	594	679	1,273	681	1,954	710	2,664	18%	18%	2,209
Research & Development	224	261	485	257	742	265	1,007	179	209	388	220	608	239	847	11%	19%	723
Other, Net	(4)	9	5	1	6	(4)	2	9	8	17	15	32	14	46	N/M	(97%)	40
Income Before Income Taxes	596	603	1,199	572	1,771	555	2,326	497	494	991	467	1,458	455	1,913	22%	22%	1,606
Income Taxes	146	148	294	140	434	136	570	122	121	243	114	357	112	469	22%	22%	393
Net Income	450	455	905	432	1,337	419	1,756	375	373	748	353	1,101	343	1,444	22%	22%	1,213
Basic Earnings per Common																	
Share–Continuing Operations	0.31	0.31	0.62	0.29	0.91	0.29	1.20	0.26	0.25	0.51	0.24	0.75	0.23	0.98	26%	22%	0.82
Diluted Earnings per Common																	
Share–Continuing Operations	0.30	0.31	0.61	0.29	0.90	0.28	1.18	0.25	0.25	0.50	0.24	0.74	0.23	0.97	22%	22%	0.82
Avg. Shares Outstanding–Basic	1,466	1,467	1,467	1,469	1,467	1,470	1,468	1,463	1,464	1,463	1,465	1,464	1,465	1,464			1,471
Avg. Shares Outstanding–Diluted	1,485	1,486	1,486	1,490	1,487	1,489	1,488	1,476	1,480	1,478	1,482	1,479	1,482	1,480			1,487
Actual Shares Outstanding	1,467	1,468	1,468	1,470	1,470	1,472	1,472	1,463	1,465	1,465	1,464	1,464	1,465	1,465			1,461

Figure 7.6
Investor Insights

The Final Word

And now, for the fifth year running, SGP's Thanksgiving Song!

Over the river and through the woods,
It's poem time again.
It's been a good year.
We wish you to hear
Our Thanksgiving Song again—Oh!

Over the river and through the woods,
Our shareholders we did treat.
Split the stock in two
And set up a new
Repurchase Plan—how neat—Oh!

Over the river and through the woods
Our star's been CLARITIN.
We know that you care
About market share
As much as non-seda-tin—Oh!

Over the river and through the woods,
With investors we did meet.
Abroad and at home
Or over the phone.
The St. Regis was quite a treat—Oh!

Over the river and through the woods,
This year in retrospect
Had lots going on
That was really très bonne
(Our French we did perfect)—Oh!

Over the river and through the woods,
Toward '98 we roam.
We thank you a lot
For supporting our stock
And promise now to end this poem!

November, 1997

pelling interest to the financial community, above and beyond what is available in the Annual Report, the *SGP Glossary*, defining medical and pharmaceutical argot on layman's terms; and *Rx Deals*, which concisely describes every major research and marketing collaboration currently underway.

In 1998 the company unveiled yet another convenient solution for busy consumers of Schering-Plough investor materials: *SPIRAL*, an acronym for Schering-Plough Investor Relations Analysts Literature.

It is a spiral-bound (thus it lies flat on a desk) compilation of critical documents: the *Investor Financial Review, Glossary*, Form 10-K, and Annual Report, with a pocket for storing the *Product Pipeline*.

What is critical to note about these publications is that they carry through the Schering-Plough style of straightforward, no-frills information, giving investors and analysts just the information they need. Even the company's Annual Report exemplifies this philosophy and practice: It is "lean and clean" in delivering the necessary information without gloss and hype. In Schering-Plough's 1998 Annual Report, for example, the state of the company's research, pharmaceutical, and health-care products divisions are all succinctly described in just ten pages. The entire document runs just thirty-six pages and has been the same length since 1993.

Schering-Plough's press releases also conform to the "lean-and-clean" philosophy. Rarely more than three pages in length, they present even the most complex update on a research project clearly, succinctly, and accurately.

MEETING MECHANICS

The other area ready for a major turnaround at Schering-Plough in the early 1990s was its meeting schedule. The company needed to expand its presence to tell its story loud and clear. Executives from headquarters, operations, and research began to participate in a variety of forums, including health-care conferences, internally organized meetings, and a regular contact program, all with the goal of increasing information about products—and most pointedly not with any intention of promoting the company for the sake of its stock. Indeed, Schering-Plough makes a point of never making any material disclosures at any meeting. Meetings are used to reinforce, not introduce, information about the company. One exception to that rule is the yearly analysts and portfolio managers meeting, when a press release summarizes highlights of the meeting and any earnings projections.

For several years before Gerry Foster came to Schering-Plough, the company held a half-day, on-site yearly meeting for analysts and portfolio managers. That meeting was held for the last time in 1990. The following year the venue moved to New York City, where, with just one exception, it has been held ever since. The meeting site was changed in response to analysts' requests for a more easily accessible location, especially for people located outside of the metropolitan area. (In 1993 Schering-Plough opened its new Drug Discovery Facility in Kenilworth, New Jersey, and it was appropriate to hold a meeting there to showcase the building.) The meetings were also shortened to include

tion to produce by 4:00 p.m. a summary of the key points raised at the

all the essential components—a financial overview and a new drug outlook—in just an hour or two. The half-day format meeting devoted to research is just not necessary every year (see Table 7.3).

In 1991 the ADAM—"A Day at Madison"—meetings were introduced. These meetings are small group sessions with fewer than thirty participants, who are invited to speak informally with key executives at Schering-Plough's executive offices in Madison, New Jersey. Three meetings are scheduled throughout the year, with analysts and portfolio managers signing up on a first-come, first-served basis. There are no formal presentations; the format is all question and answer. Executives participating in ADAM include the president/COO, the CFO, the treasurer, and senior representatives from the company's operating and research divisions. The group then meets the chairman/CEO for lunch. The meetings conclude around 1:30 P.M., at which time investor relations and corporate communications staff snap into action to produce by 4:00 P.M. a summary of the key points raised at the

Table 7.3
SGP Annual Participation in Meetings

Meeting Type	Format	Speaker(s)
SGP Analysts and Portfolio Managers Meeting	Lunch, Keynote Address, Q&A	CEO Senior Executives Available
ADAM (A Day at Madison)	Q&A Only	CEO and Senior Executives
Brokerage-Sponsored Conferences	Speeches/Q&A	CEO, COO, CFO, Treasurer and SVP IR
AIMR and EFFAS Conferences	Speeches/Q&A	SVP IR and Treasurer
Investor Relations Association Blue Chip Meetings	Speeches/Q&A	SVP IR
European Meetings	Speeches/Q&A	CEO and Various Executives
Marketing Trips	Informal Presentations/ Q&A	SVP IR , Treasurer and IR Staff

meeting. This summary is called, appropriately, *ADAM's RIB*, or *A Day at Madison's Review in Brief.*

In 1999 Schering-Plough investor relations will participate in more than 100 meetings, including its yearly analysts and portfolio managers meeting and the three ADAM gatherings. The rest of the meetings are brokerage-sponsored pharmaceutical conferences, professional association gatherings (such as the AIMR), and marketing road trips. For the latter, members of the investor relations department travel to major cities throughout the year to meet with investors on an individual or small-group basis, and make several forays to European cities as well.

Schering-Plough also sponsors a quarterly earnings conference call, although it is an experience quite different from the ordinary. When the company decided to initiate conference calls, the IR department surveyed the investment community and discovered that many felt too much time was spent listening to other analysts grandstanding in front of clients and generally wasting time. So, beginning in January 1996, Schering-Plough notified the investment community that they were invited to participate in the SGP QUIC call—Quarterly Update, Information and Comment. These reviews last just ten minutes and are one-way only. The response to these sessions has been overwhelmingly positive—and appreciative.

In addition, investors can access Schering-Plough's quarterly earnings releases—and all press releases—as well as financial information on the company's Web page. Also on the Internet site are documents such as the Annual Report, 10-K and 10-Q reports, and histories of share repurchases, stock splits, and dividend increases.

MAKING MORE OF LESS

Schering-Plough is a company that puts its money where its mouth is when it comes to serving its investors. The company is proud of the relationships it has built over the years with the investment community, and is always on the lookout for new ways to communicate the good news about Schering-Plough's performance today and what lies ahead for the future. Top management support, a lean, motivated staff, and a strong message conveyed consistently and credibly are a winning combination for Schering-Plough's investor relations program.

8

The Strategic Role of Corporate Financial Communications and Investor Relations at BASF

Klaus D. Jessen

In the mid-1980s BASF senior management recognized the need to further improve its partnership with the financial and investment community. Even with a generally positive view of the future due to its recent strong financial performance, there was a growing uneasiness among senior management that the public perception of BASF and its activities were incomplete and inaccurate. Comments by institutional investors, financial analysts, investment bankers, and articles in the financial press, complemented by market research initiated by the company, suggested that few people had a clear vision of the BASF Group and its widely diversified activities. The existence of naphtha crackers for the production of ethylene and propylene may have contributed to the misperception of BASF as a predominantly basic chemical company. The reality, of course, was that in this vertically integrated organization such feedstock was consumed primarily by internal operations, and corresponding profits contributed to overall earnings performance.

Beyond its home market, BASF management was confronted with another perception problem. People either did not know the company and its name or they reacted with comments such as, "BASF, oh yes, the tape people." It was true that magnetic tapes were, in fact, the most visible BASF product for international consumers who happened to purchase quality audio or video cassettes. However, that business represented only 2 percent of total group sales, and was fully divested by the end of 1996.

The apparent wrong perception of the company's main activities led management to suspect that this might be one of the reasons for the undervaluation of the company's shares on international stock exchanges. Various publications from leading international financial analysts supported the assumption that the fair value of the company was not reflected in the company's stock price at the time. This growing awareness of a gap between the "real BASF" and the perception held by a significant and influential segment of the population led senior management to define a clear strategic target: BASF had to establish itself in the minds of the international financial community as one of the world's leading chemical corporations with a broad but focused product range, production sites in thirty-nine countries, and sales activities in more than 170 countries. This was the catalyst for the creation of an investor relations department, as is discussed later in the section, "Commitment of BASF Management to Investor Relations."

COMPANY BACKGROUND

Badische Anilin und Soda Fabrik A.G. (now known as BASF) was founded in 1865 along the banks of the Rhine River. BASF was one of the first companies to manufacture dyes from coal tar, later on specializing, for example, in a bright bluish purple dye known as indigo.[1] Diversification into organic chemicals and new production facilities in Ludwigshafen were made possible by the profits generated by their dye business.

After World War II, growth at BASF proceeded at a brisk pace and has taken a three-pronged approach: vertical integration, global expansion, and an increasing emphasis on noncyclical products. Vertical integration provides reliable, low-cost feedstock to its downstream operations. The upstream activities of BASF include, for example, production of ethylene, propylene, ammonia, and acetylene, all-in-all representing about two-thirds of the approximately 300 "immortal" basic chemicals that are the building blocks for modern chemistry. In the mid-1960s BASF decided to go abroad, either by establishing new production sites—in some cases as joint ventures—or by acquiring companies on a worldwide scale. Seeking to gain access to the world's largest chemical market and avoid tariffs, the company formed a number of U.S. partnerships. Due to large acquisitions, especially in 1985 in the United States (Inmont, American Enka, and three Celanese subsidiaries), BASF North America sales grew to $5 billion, with more than 90 percent of sales coming from local production.

In addition, BASF has sought to diversify into noncyclical products with crop protection agents and pharmaceuticals as well as coatings and paints. The company is investing 4 to 5 percent of sales in research and development annually and has moved away from commodity chemicals and toward specialty chemical products. The most recent move into the European distribution of natural gas will substantially reduce earnings volatility.

BASF—CURRENT

In 1990 BASF celebrated its 125th anniversary. In remarks prepared for the occasion, Hans Albers, board chairman (1983–1990) observed

The goals expressed in *Chemistry Looks to the Future* can only be achieved if we have clear objectives, if we are resolved to affirm and participate in the changes around us. Our international thinking and dealing represents a reliable basis for BASF's further expansion in an increasingly international arena of competition. Being active in future-oriented markets, BASF is prepared to meet the growing and changing demand.[2]

Senior management has developed certain strategies, goals, and guidelines to achieve a competitive edge in the 1990s. BASF's Vision 2010 states

- We are recognized worldwide as a successful, innovative, transnational company in the chemical industry.
- We are achieving a high return on the capital employed.
- Core competencies characterize our portfolio.
- Our market is the world.
- BASF is the preferred partner of its customers.

The corporate guidelines are as follows:

- Our objective is to work as a partner with our customers to achieve long-term customer satisfaction. Within BASF, we cooperate across all geographical and organizational boundaries to accomplish this goal.
- We employ modern logistic systems to ensure the smooth flow of products and merchandise between regions.
- We conduct research and development internationally in accordance with the needs of local markets and customers.
- We create competence centers, taking advantage of all opportunities for synergy, including joint projects with universities and other companies.
- We use our leading position to help share scientific and technological progress, identifying new business opportunities and exploiting synergistic effects arising from our integrated research.

STRUCTURE, OPERATIONS, PRODUCTS

Table 8.1 summarizes the organization of BASF in July 1999. Seventeen operating divisions manage a diversified product portfolio which is geographically dispersed over twelve regional divisions worldwide. Sixteen corporate and functional divisions provide support and assistance to BASF Group operations around the globe.

Table 8.2 provides a ten-year summary (1989–1998) of selected BASF Group performance data. Even as the company was celebrating its 125th anniversary, the rapid growth and profitability of the 1980s was giving way to the turbulent, troubled 1990s. A severe worldwide chemical industry slump, overcapacity, and fierce competition from low-cost-producing countries combined to produce the disappointing results shown from 1990 to 1993. Later, recession and the unanticipated social, political, and economic costs of reunification drove BASF and other German companies even deeper in a downward spiral.

The year 1994 saw a significant improvement in BASF operations and financial performance, due in part to an upturn in the chemical industry that contributed to an 8-percent increase in sales. In addition, restructuring, downsizing, and other cost reductions produced a turnaround in 1994 profitability (BASF reduced its employee base by over 31,000 since 1989, a 23-percent reduction). Even with the general improvement of the business climate in the years 1995 through 1998, restructuring efforts continued to strengthen the BASF product portfolio and the regional presence with investments in capital expenditures, strategic acquisitions, and divestitures, as well as in research and development (see Table 8.2).

COMMITMENT OF BASF MANAGEMENT TO INVESTOR RELATIONS

The most essential support for an active and progressive investor relations program is the commitment from a company's top management. BASF's chief financial officer found a receptive audience as he approached his colleagues on the board of executive directors. His recommendations to initiate an active corporate financial communications policy were supported by the board and plans were made to establish an investor relations department. It should be noted, however, that such a substantial broadening in a company's communications strategy in the conservative environment of Germany required considerable powers of persuasion.

In late 1987 and early 1988 BASF created a one-man investor relations department, which was soon to be increased by the addition of an assistant investor relations manager and a full-time secretary. The author, selected to become BASF's first investor relations manager, brought to the position a strong international background, long-term experience in financial and accounting matters, fluency in several languages, and a solid knowledge of the group's worldwide structure.

Once the decision to establish an active corporate financial communications program was made and an investor relations department had been established, gaining internal credibility was the predominant immediate task. Managing directors of BASF Group's seventeen operating divisions had to be convinced of the advantages derived from an active investor relations program. Therefore, the investor relations manager set out to visit all operating divisions of the BASF Group. Each operating division is managed as a profit center for its corresponding product portfolio, carrying, therefore, responsibility for the individual divisional profitability (see Table 8.1).

Gaining the support of BASF's operating divisions was essential if corporate financial communications activities were to be successful. Not only did the divisions need to provide data on operations and financial performance, but managing directors, on many occasions headed by the chief executive officer, the chief financial officer, and the president of the finance division, would be included among a group of speakers representing BASF on various external and internal occasions. Among external audiences, these top managers would be talking to institutional and private investors, financial analysts, and equity consultants from universal banks.

The investor relations manager was successful in gaining vital divisional support. One of the major potential benefits of an active investor relations program that proved to be persuasive in winning the support of divisional management was the enormous potential for the creation of shareholder value.

Divisional management agreed to provide essential facts and figures on divisional business operations, capital expenditures, research and development, and so on. Division managers also made a commitment to participate as speakers, representing BASF to various external and internal audiences. To assist them in their public presentations and appearances, an investor relations handbook was prepared and made available to all speakers.

MARKET RESEARCH AND INTERNAL CONSULTING

With the board's decision to establish an active investor relations program, the job of launching an international communications activity had just begun. Starting a corporate financial communications pro-

Table 8.1
BASF Group Overview

Board of Executive Directors	Operating Divisions		Regional Divisions		Corporate Divisions, Functional Divisions*	
Ressort I *Strube* Chairman					ZR	Legal, Taxes & Insurance — *Sünner*
					ZZ	Planning & Controlling — *Frommer*
						interdivisional negotiating teams — *Feldmann*
Ressort II *Voscherau*	AD	Fertilizers — *Kreimeyer*	LM	Southern Europe — *Bach*	ZH	Main Laboratory — *Küsters*
	AP	Crop Protection — *Vogel, F.*	LN	Northern Europe — *Stickings*		
	ME	Fine Chemicals — *Dudeck*	LZ	Central Europe — *Thoma-schewski*		
	MP	Pharmaceuticals — *Spickschen*				
Ressort III *Kley* Deputy Chairman	EC	Coatings — *Löbbe*	LR	Eastern Europe, Africa, West Asia — *Werwie*	ZF	Finance — *Müller, E.*
	RM	Oil & Gas — *Detharding*				
	RR	Raw Materials Purchasing — *Mörike*				
Ressort IV *Trautz*	KS	Styrenic Polymers — *Prätorius*	LC	East Asia — *Binckli*	ZK	Polymers Laboratory — *Schenck*
	KT	Engineering Plastics — *Schmitt, B.* from 1.8.99: *Baumgartner*	LJ	Japan — *Nissen*		
	KU	Polyurethanes — *Dhanis*	LS	South East Asia/ Australia — *Burgert*		

Ressort	Code	Department	Name	Code	Department	Name	Code	Department	Name
Ressort V *Becks*							**ZI** *DL	Corporate Engineering Logistics	*Anderlohr* *Flickinger*
							*DP *DU	Human Resources Environment, Safety & Energy	*Dehmel* *Seufert*
							*DW	BASF AG Works Engineering	*Buhr*
Ressort VI *Hambrecht*	**CI** **CZ**	Industrial Chemicals Intermediates	*Strickler* *Lach*				**ZA** *WA	Ammonia Laboratory Antwerp Works	*Degner* *Dieusaert*
	RC	Petrochemicals & Inorganics	*Niess*						
Ressort VII *Oakley*	**KF**	Fiber Products	*Hapke*	**LB** **NC**	South America North America Chemicals	*Acker* *Jennings*	***NT**	North America Finance	*Bock*
				NL	North America Coatings & Colorants	*McKulka*			
				NP	North America Polymers	*Lizzi*			
				NV	North America Consumer Products & Life Science	*Kast*			
Ressort VIII *Marcinowski* Research Executive Director	**ED** **EF** **ES**	Dispersions Colorants Specialty Chemicals	*Kohnle* *Gramlich* *Riedmüller*				**ZD**	Colorants Laboratory	*Paul*

Table 8.2
Ten-Year Summary, BASF Group

Million DM	1989	1990	1991	1992	1993	1994	1995	1996	1997	1998
Sales and earnings										
Sales	46,163	45,043	44,556	41,933	40,568	43,674	46,229	48,776	55,780	54,065
Income from operations	4,329	2,755	2,180	1,311	1,032	2,149	4,023	4,293	5,342	5,132
Profit before taxes	4,384	2,747	2,110	1,239	1,058	2,111	4,128	4,414	5,331	5,419
Net income	2,030	1,111	1,056	613	761	1,170	2,423	2,839	3,205	3,255
Net income after taxes and minority interest	2,015	1,107	1,039	615	858	1,284	2,471	2,790	3,236	3,324
Capital expenditures and depreciation										
Additions to fixed assets	4,379	5,098	5,381	5,730	4,423	3,274	5,363	6,864	5,798	8,079
Depreciation of fixed assets	3,043	3,293	3,463	3,541	3,342	4,380	3,687	3,666	4,005	4,460
Number of employees										
At year-end*	136,990	134,647	129,434	123,254	112,020	106,266	106,565	105,589	104,979	105,945
Key data										
Net icome per share (DM)	3.54	1.94	1.82	1.08	1.49	2.15	4.05	4.54	5.22	5.34
Cash flow	5,520	5,024	4,765	4,451	4,635	5,565	6,368	6,798	7,225	7,258
Return on sales before income taxes and interest expenses (%)	10.6	7.3	5.9	4.3	3.8	6.0	9.9	10.0	10.4	11.0
Return on assets before income taxes and interest expenses (%)	14.4	9.2	7.1	4.7	3.9	6.5	11.2	11.4	12.6	11.9
Return on equity after taxes (%)	15.3	7.8	7,3	4.2	5.2	7.6	14.3	14.8	14.6	13.2

gram that would meet professional standards from the very beginning would not have been possible without external guidance and knowledgeable support. Instead of hiring a well-known corporate financial communications consulting firm, BASF decided to approach leading investor relations practitioners. Long before research in "best industry practices" became fashionable, the investor relations department arranged meetings with six American chemical and pharmaceutical companies, including DuPont, Schering-Plough, and American Cyanamid, among others. All American companies approached by BASF enjoyed outstanding reputations for their excellence in corporate financial communications.

In preparing for individual interviews, BASF developed a detailed and thorough questionnaire covering a wide range of investor relations topics. To their surprise, the visiting team from Germany received a warm and friendly reception from all of their discussion partners. All questions were answered in an open and frank manner, even though BASF would eventually be competing for the favor of the same institutional investors and financial analysts.

Returning from their U.S. trip, the BASF team prepared a summary of their market research on best industry practices in corporate financial communications. This synthesis was to serve as a fundamental platform for BASF's investor relations concept and strategy. Major conclusions emerging from this synthesis of interviews were

- To start investor relations activities immediately in the global financial triad, making presentations to leading financial markets in Europe, North America, and Asia.
- To achieve high-quality standards by having the executives represent the company in external presentations, providing the financial community with quality information in terms of segmental disclosure.
- To watch carefully some of the fundamental principles of investor relations activity, such as the principle of continuity and the principle of credibility.

This approach to investor relations won the enthusiastic support of BASF top management, who gave the "green light" to go ahead with the preparation and organization of an international schedule. It should be noted that this market-research exercise was repeated two years later in the United Kingdom with the same successful results. Six leading U.K. chemical and pharmaceutical companies, including ICI, Glaxo, Wellcome, and BP Chemicals were approached by the BASF team, this time with two years of investor relations experience guiding their market-research efforts. The outcome of the U.K. meetings basically confirmed the investor relations concept and strategy formulated two years earlier.

ORGANIZATION OF INVESTOR RELATIONS AT BASF

Due to its origins and its ultimate goal to reduce the cost of capital, the investor relations function was established as a new organizational unit within the central finance division (see Figure 8.1). The most appropriate organizational assignment of the investor relations department is always determined within the context of a corporation's individual structures. As the cost of capital comprises the cost of equity and the cost of liabilities to the capital market, the BASF investor relations department has also assumed responsibilities for the relationship with international rating agencies. The fundamental research on group performance, strategies, operational developments, and financial highlights is based on the same BASF data that are used for external publications and communications.

External target groups addressed by the investor relations department include

- institutional investors
- private shareholders
- financial analysts
- equity consultants in banks
- holders of bonds and commercial papers (via rating agencies)
- the academic community (university professors, students, etc.)

The only important target group not addressed directly by BASF investor relations are financial and economic journalists, who are served mainly through the public relations department. But even in this case investor relations is involved indirectly, as an increasing number of journalists prefer to quote leading financial analysts as their chief sources when they prepare articles on individual companies.

Organizational integration of investor relations is achieved by close cooperation with the strategic planning department, the accounting department, and the controllers of the seventeen operating divisions. Operating divisions provide investor relations with the lifeblood of corporate financial communications—strategic views combined with financial facts and figures. Organizational and technical support for presentations at individual locations is also given by finance managers or public relations officers from group subsidiaries.

ROLE OF INVESTOR RELATIONS AT BASF

In his "Letter to Shareholders" in the 1992 Annual Report, Dr. Jürgen Strube, chairman of the board of executive directors of BASF, outlined

Figure 8.1
Organization of BASF Central Finance Division

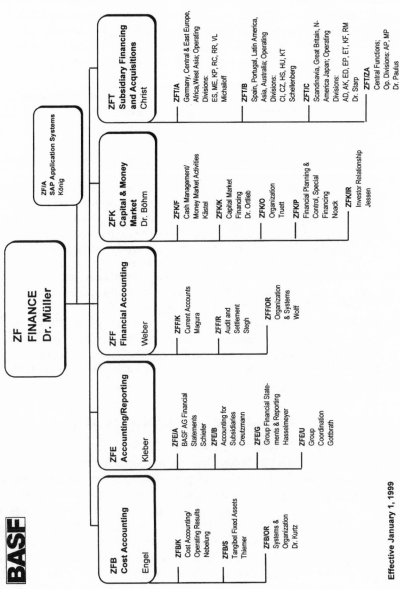

BASF

ZF
FINANCE
Dr. Müller

ZF/A
SAP Application Systems
König

ZFB
Cost Accounting
Engel

ZFB/K
Cost Accounting/
Operating Results
Nebelung

ZFB/S
Tangibel Fixed Assets
Thiemer

ZFB/OR
Systems &
Organization
Dr. Kurtz

ZFE
Accounting/Reporting
Kleber

ZFE/A
BASF AG Financial
Statements
Schiefer

ZFE/B
Accounting for
Subsidiaries
Creutzmann

ZFE/G
Group Financial State-
ments & Reporting
Hasselmeyer

ZFE/U
Group
Coordination
Gottbrath

ZFF
Financial Accounting
Weber

ZFF/K
Current Accounts
Magura

ZFF/R
Audit and
Settlement
Stegh

ZFF/OR
Organization
& Systems
Wolff

ZFK
Capital & Money
Market
Dr. Böhm

ZFK/F
Cash Management/
Money Market Activities
Kästel

ZFK/K
Capital Market
Financing
Dr. Ortlieb

ZFK/O
Organization
Truett

ZFK/P
Financial Planning &
Control, Special
Financing
Noack

ZFK/IR
Investor Relationship
Jessen

ZFT
Subsidiary Financing
and Acquisitions
Christ

ZFT/A
Germany, Central & East Europe,
Africa, West Asia; Operating
Divisions:
ES, ME, KP, RC, RR, VL
Michailoff

ZFT/B
Spain, Portugal, Latin America,
Asia, Australia; Operating
Divisions:
CI, CZ, HS, HU, KT
Schellenberg

ZFT/C
Scandinavia, Great Britain, N-
America Japan; Operating
Divisions:
AD, AK, ED, EP, ET, KF, RM
Dr. Starp

ZFT/ZA
Central Functions;
Op. Divisions: AP, MP
Dr. Paulus

Effective January 1, 1999

the mission and objective of the company's investor relations program: "Our Investor Relations Program is aimed at investors, financial analysts and banks both in Germany and abroad. The objective is to internationalize our shareholder base with a view to improving the valuation of the BASF share in the long term."[3] Six years later, in the 1998 Annual Report, Chairman Strube reported, "We take active steps to provide investors and financial analysts with candid information about our company's progress. . . . Quarterly reporting was expanded in 1998."[4]

Three themes emerge from these ongoing communications to shareholders and members of the financial community:

1. The BASF share is still undervalued.

2. BASF is actively seeking to internationalize their shareholder base. From the very inception of BASF's communication activities, management decided to initiate an international investor relations program. One of the main reasons for this was that in the German equity market the relative weighting of chemical shares represents about 12 to 13 percent of total market capitalization. BASF, as one of the three major German chemical companies, was already represented in nearly every deposit account of German institutional investors and also held by almost 300,000 private shareholders. The only way to identify potential new shareholders was to go "abroad," addressing the financial community in the leading financial centers of Europe, North America, and Asia.

3. BASF is seeking a long-term shareholder commitment. This emphasis on the long term is a common guideline, underlying and running throughout BASF Group strategies, investment policies, research and development expenditures, and investor relations activities—virtually the entire strategic and operational fabric of the company.

INVESTOR RELATIONS ACTIVITIES

In turn, these mission statements, objectives, and emerging themes set the tone and established the parameters for BASF investor relations activities. Initial company presentations were scheduled in European capital cities where BASF shares were already listed on national stock exchanges. These included London, Amsterdam, Brussels, Paris, Zurich, Geneva, and Vienna. Additional locations with a proven record of significant investment in foreign shares like Milan, Stockholm, Edinburgh, Glasgow, and Dublin were then chosen. In North America, New York City, Boston, and Toronto were selected to be visited each year, with annual road shows also scheduled for Tokyo, Hong Kong, and Singapore.

From time to time BASF accepts additional invitations to present the company, either for a second time in one of the financial centers mentioned or at additional locations where they meet important institutional investors on a one-to-one basis. When showing up for a second or even third time at one financial center (e.g., London), BASF is very careful to avoid the risk of "overkill." Therefore, they accept invitations only once every three months, when new quarterly figures have been published in interim reports and discussed in corresponding press conferences and analyst meetings. Over the years, BASF's international program has generated substantial additional interest from portfolio managers, especially in Anglo-Saxon countries, which is also reflected in the increased number of one-on-one investors meetings at corporate headquarters in Ludwigshafen.

For their investor relations presentations in every leading financial center, BASF selects a prominent universal bank, investment bank, or brokerage house as a main sponsor. In some countries BASF uses a group of two or three institutions on a rotating basis. The main responsibilities of a sponsor include the invitation of target groups, follow-up marketing to these events by phone calls or a second mailing, the organization of the conference or round-table meeting, and the provision of feedback on the presentation, collecting the opinions of participants on the content and quality of the meeting. Whenever BASF feels comfortable with the support it receives from their main sponsor in a country, they follow the old principle of "don't change a winning team." Frequently, BASF investor relations activities constitute only one of several other cooperative business relationships with a sponsoring institution, which helps to motivate sponsors to provide their best efforts.

Investor relations presentations are made at all important financial centers at least once a year, in "good times and in bad." The investment community clearly welcomed BASF's willingness to "show up" in bad times and openly discuss company earnings and business performance in the years 1990 to 1993. Company spokespersons explained the reasons for declining results and told analysts what strategic moves management had initiated to counter the decline. Certainly these difficult years in the early 1990s were part of an overall industry downturn within the context of a macroeconomic scenario of a worldwide recession. Declining capacity utilization and strong pressure on selling prices led to poor results in some of BASF's product portfolios. Rigid cost control of fixed costs in combination with positive earnings performance in other operational segments helped BASF to offset somewhat these negative developments. However, according to the author's personal experience, it may be noted that

Analysts are not interested in yesterday's performance, they are [primarily] interested in your performance today as an indication of your future performance.... Instead of concentrating too much on detailed figures, analysts are much more interested in strategies—segment strategies, investment strategies, product strategies, R&D strategies. Analysts want to know what strategic approaches [the company will take] at different levels of corporate activity because they already have some idea of what the financial outcomes will be from other sources—competitors, average of industry, etc.... Of course your [strategic intentions] are compared with real performance 6–12 months hence, to see if your promises/expectations were really fulfilled. If your strategic indications correspond with following through with real performance, you add increased credibility to your strategic statements.[5]

Another interesting and innovative approach to corporate financial communications is the development of a practice at BASF known as "shadow-boxing." From the outset of its corporate financial communications program, BASF has viewed communications as a two-way street, not just a one-way interaction from the information source inside the company to the financial community outside. Especially on the occasion of strategic background discussions with leading financial analysts, managing directors may engage in shadow-boxing, discussing possible strategic scenarios with experienced analysts who frequently have visited other "friendly competitors" worldwide. In some cases outside analysts help to identify critical areas where management attention has already been given but which might, at least temporarily, require more focus.

In recognition of their progressive and innovation activities in the field of corporate financial communications, in 1990 BASF was selected to receive the first European Investor Relations Prize, awarded by the economic magazine *WirtschaftsWoche*. A total of approximately sixty leading European countries submitted documented files on their investor relations activities, which were then evaluated by a grand jury composed of a broad spectrum of portfolio managers, financial analysts, and IR consultants. In the end, BASF emerged as the winner. The winner's cup is now proudly displayed in the center of the round table located in the investor relations office, where meetings are held with institutional and private investors, financial analysts, university students, and other external groups.

MEASURING THE SUCCESS OF BASF'S IR PROGRAM

Despite the favorable share-price development in recent years, the author has cautioned, "The first lesson for anybody who is active in the communication business is the wisdom that efforts will only pay [off] in the medium and longer term. One should not expect short-term miracles with regard to share price developments, as fundamental promising developments may be jeopardized by macro-economic downturns, currency turbulences or political turmoil."[6]

If share price is not an appropriate yardstick to measure the effectiveness of corporate financial communications (at least in the short run), what other criteria should be used to evaluate the quality and progress in a company's investor relations program? BASF has developed the following criteria to measure the improvements made in their communications activities:

General Corporate Awareness

Making BASF known in the international financial community was the primary task of the investor relations program when it was started in late 1987 and early 1988. From the very beginning it was deemed important to create a general corporate awareness of BASF as one additional "friendly competitor" in the competition for funds in the premier investment league.

Structural Knowledge

BASF is a leading international chemical group with a broad variety in its product spectrum, ranging from crude oil and natural gas to sophisticated products like pharmaceuticals and vitamins. Knowledge of the fundamental structure of BASF's operational activities in seventeen operating divisions, grouped into five segments for reporting purposes, is essential to understand the underlying strategies and to evaluate the earnings potential in each of BASF's segments. The information on corporate activities is communicated to the general public by the public relations department and the investor relations department, differentiating their responsibilities according to their target audiences.

Quality of Investors' Audiences

When BASF started their investor relations presentations several years ago, they were quite pleased to see 100 people assembled in one of London's impressive Guild Halls. Later, as BASF explored participants' real interest in the company and in purchasing their shares, they began to suspect that some of their guests had attended primarily to enjoy a free lunch. Measuring the responsiveness of an IR invitation just in absolute terms of the number of participants can lead to misleading conclusions.

Abandoning the numbers game (total audience size), BASF began an ABC analysis of potential and actual institutional investors (A stands for top investors, B for medium-size investors, C for investors with potential to grow into B or A). This analysis is based on investors' own periodic publications or other reports available in economic magazines and newspapers. This enables BASF to review a list of institutional investors—prepared, for example, by the sponsor of an event.

Quality and Frequency of Research Reports

When starting their investor relations activities in the late 1980s, only a small number of financial analysts published research reports on BASF, and this primarily happened on a sporadic basis. The institutionalization of financial corporate communications in BASF's investor relations department has allowed the company to enter into a dialogue with leading chemical analysts. In turn, financial analysts are offered a cooperative service, as they have the opportunity to transmit draft versions of their research reports to the BASF investor relations department. There, an internal company team assists external analysts in the strategic description and development of BASF's businesses and the fundamental analysis of important product portfolios within various operating divisions.

As a consequence of the existence and the cooperative services offered, the total number of financial analysts continuously following the development of the BASF Group has increased significantly in recent years (the current estimate is approximately 150). In addition, the frequency of updated reports, at least on a quarterly basis, has also increased significantly. Finally, the fundamental analysis of BASF's operational activities has also improved in most reports in terms of quality and strategic understanding.

Evaluation of Print Information

External feedback on the quality and expressiveness of BASF printed information (i.e., annual reports and quarterly interim statements) is another measure of the effectiveness of its investor relations activities. In a comparative survey of German corporations conducted by an academic team from a leading German university, BASF's management report in the Annual Report received the highest appreciation with regard to the informative quality and the strategic insight into the company.

However, while these five criteria are important measurements of the effectiveness of an investor relations program, they do not compensate for a company's performance. The best communications skills and efforts can only achieve their optimum effects in the context of a convincing "strategic story" of the corporation. In the environment of a disappointing operating performance, communications can support investors' long-term confidence and thereby limit downward pressure on share prices.

PREPARING FOR THE NEXT MILLENNIUM

Improvement in Segmental Reporting

Starting in 1995, BASF significantly improved its quarterly reports and the segmental information of the separate operational activities. The company now reports net sales as well as income from operations for each of the five operating segments every three months, and publishes a profit and loss account as well as a balance sheet for the entire BASF Group.

Share Buy Back

BASF shareholders have approved the decision of the company's Annual General Meeting in May 1998 to authorize management to buy back the company's own shares. Based on a new German capital-market law, corporations are entitled to buy back up to 10 percent of their own shares over a maximum period of eighteen months. This represents another attempt in Germany to harmonize its capital market structures with similar established mechanisms in Anglo-Saxon countries.

The major reason for BASF to buy back its own shares is to optimize its capital structure, as the equity to total assets ratio at the end of 1998 reached 50 percent. With equity being the most expensive source of financing for a corporation, this capital structure is suboptimal. Therefore, BASF will primarily use its own cash reserves to buy back its shares, cancel the shares, and offset the purchase price paid from equity. Through this procedure, BASF will obtain several advantages: The total balance sheet will be shortened by the amount invested in the buy back of shares, the ratios calculated on either equity or on total assets will improve, and earnings per share will increase due to the reduced number of outstanding and voting shares.

In addition, BASF implemented a stock-option program for top management as well as an employee shareholder plan. Both programs require a direct and individual investment by the participants. At the Annual General Meeting on April 29, 1999, a stock-option program for roughly 1,200 BASF managers worldwide was approved by the shareholders. This stock-option program may be exercised for three years following a three-year vesting period, whereby two benchmarks will define the execution of options. First, the share price of BASF must increase at least 30 percent in comparison to the issue share price, and second, the performance of the BASF share price must exceed the performance of the EURO STOXX index. This stock-option program will further align and strengthen the common interest between shareholders and the management of the corporation.

Listing on the New York Stock Exchange

BASF is currently preparing to list its shares on the most important stock exchange in the world, the New York Stock Exchange, in the year 2000. By making its shares on international capital markets even more visible and transparent, BASF management intends to increase American shareholding in the corporation substantially over the next years.

Consequently, top management will engage itself even more in direct communications with fund managers and financial analysts in order to position the BASF share to the maximum extent possible in the minds of the American investment community. The chief executive officer, the deputy chairman, and chief financial officer, as well as the chairman of BASF Corporation, Mount Olive (who is also a board member of BASF AG), will be involved heavily in these increased efforts to position BASF within the American investment community. With the support of a leading American investment bank as well as an additional investor relations public relations agency, BASF intends to increase its efforts toward institutional fund managers and financial analysts.

As the intended listing on the New York Stock Exchange also requires a change in accounting systems, BASF decided to change to US-GAAP in 1998. Based on the two years of GAAP accounting and reporting (1998 and 1999), the listing on the "big board" is expected toward the end of the first half of the year 2000. Investor relations efforts targeted at the American investment community will definitely continue after the listing, as fund managers and financial analysts will require a continuous dialogue with top management in order to receive appropriate information on all material operational aspects and financial items of BASF.

BASF sees the need to target analysts worldwide. Their published recommendation can play a role if, for example, a huge acquisition were to cause BASF to tap the international capital market with a new primary issue. Simultaneously, BASF continues to work on improving its relationships with leading international rating agencies, where they already benefit from top ratings in the long-term (AA) and the short-term (A 1 plus) categories.

The strategic role of investor relations and corporate communications is clearly to prepare a solid ground for the financing requirements of tomorrow and thereafter. Because strategic credibility cannot be built in a day or a month or a year, a long-term perspective and commitment continue to guide BASF as it looks to the future. If the past is any predictor of the future, BASF should remain one of the world's most important and successful companies for many years to come.[7]

NOTES

1. "BASF A.G.," in *International Directory of Company Histories*, vol. 1 (Detroit: St. James Press, 1988), 305–308.

2. BASF Milestones in Its History (company document, 1990).

3. BASF, *1992 Annual Report*, 3.

4. BASF, *1998 Annual Report*, 5.

5. Klaus D. Jessen, interview by Richard B. Higgins, 22 June 1992, Ludwigshafen, Germany.

6. Klaus D. Jessen, May 1995.

7. "BASF A.G.," 307.

9

Reuters PLC:
A Global Information Wholesaler
to the Financial Community

Peter Gregson and Geoffrey Wicks

Reuters is a very old company in a very young business, one that has been largely created in the past two to three decades. But in one major respect Reuters is the same as it was in 1850. When Paul Julius Reuter started, he used carrier pigeons to carry stock market prices between Brussels and Aachen. His customers were professionals, paying for the information they needed.

Today, Reuters still supplies and delivers financial information and related products and services. Its customers are still professionals. But Reuters was transformed during the last quarter of the twentieth century through some bold pioneering ventures that created a range of electronic information products for the world's rapidly growing financial markets. The development of new technology enabled it to build a global business as a wholesaler to the financial community, supplying information electronically and the related products and services used to deliver, manage, and deal with information.

General

- Reuters supplies the global business and the news media with the widest range of information and news products, including real-time financial data; transaction and risk-management systems; numerical, textual, historical, and graphical databases; and news, news video, and news pictures. Reuters designs and installs trading-room systems. It extensively uses Internet technology for wider distribution of information and news outside trading rooms.

- Some 498,500 users in 57,900 locations access Reuters information and news worldwide. Data are provided for more than 400,000 shares, bonds, and financial instruments. There are more than 2 million Reuters codes.

- Financial information is obtained from 267 exchanges and over-the-counter markets, and supplied by some 4,980 clients who subscribe to Reuters.

- Reuters is the world's largest news and television agency, with 2,072 journalists, photographers, and cameramen in 182 bureaus serving 157 countries. News is gathered and edited for both business and media clients in twenty-two languages. Approximately 1.5 to 2 million words are transmitted daily. Some 292 subscribers plus their networks and affiliates in ninety-three countries use Reuters television news coverage.

- Reuters services are delivered to clients over the world's most extensive global private satellite and cable communications network. At peak time, Reuters updates 2,000 prices and other data per second, with 50 million changes handled daily.

- As of December 31, 1998, the group employed 16,938 staff in 218 cities in ninety-six countries.

Financial

- Reuters is one of the largest companies quoted on the London Stock Exchange, with a market capitalization of approximately £13.5 billion (see Table 9.1).

International Market Leader

Reuters's position as an international market leader is based on the following:

- A worldwide information and news reporting network known for speed, accuracy, integrity, and impartiality.

- A constantly developing communications network and a product line distinguished by its breadth and quality.

- Comprehensive financial databases for both real-time and historical information.

- A proven reputation for reliability and continuous technological innovation.

Reuters's Independence

Reuters is a public company with shareholders throughout the world. The share structure has been designed to guarantee the company's independence and integrity. There is a single Founders

Table 9.1
Reuters Information, 1989–1998

	1998	1997	1996	1995	1994	1993	1992	1991	1990	1989
Revenue (£m)	3,032	2,882	2,914	2,703	2,309	1,874	1,568	1,467	1,369	1,187
Profit before tax after amortization (£m)	580	626	652	558	510	440	383	340	320	283
Earnings per ordinary share (p)	26.7	24.0	27.3	23.2	21.7	18.0	14.0	13.7	12.4	10.9
Dividends per ordinary share (p)	14.40	13.00	11.75	9.80	8.00	6.50	5.30	4.25	3.75	3.25

Share, which has an overriding vote if there is a threat to the company's independence. Furthermore, no shareholder is allowed to acquire 15 percent or more of the ordinary shares.

The Reuters Founders Share Company Limited

The Reuters Founders Share Company was set up in 1984 to safeguard the neutrality and independence of Reuters. The Reuter trustees, as directors of the Reuters Founders Share Company, have the power to prevent any group or individual from gaining a controlling share of the company. They also have a duty to ensure that the Reuter Trust Principles are observed.

Directors of the Founders Share Company are the trustees of Reuters. The Founders Share also protects the Reuter Trust Principles, which state the following:

- That Reuters should at no time pass into the hands of any one interest, group, or faction.
- That the integrity, independence, and freedom from bias of Reuters shall at all times be fully preserved.
- That Reuters shall supply unbiased and reliable news services to newspapers, news agencies, broadcasters, and other media subscribers and to businesses, governments, institutions, individuals, and others with whom Reuters has or may have contracts.
- That Reuters shall pay due regard to the many interests it serves in addition to those of the media.
- That no effort shall be spared to expand, develop and adapt the news and other services and products of Reuters so as to maintain its leading position in the international news and information business.

REUTERS CORPORATE STRUCTURE

Board of Directors	Chairman, six other nonexecutive directors, and six executive directors.
Group Executive Committee	Senior corporate management group chaired by chief executive; includes finance director, four other executive directors, company secretary, and director of human resources.
Transition Steering Committee	Responsible for the planning and implementation of the company's new corporate structure, announced July 1998 to go into effect January 1, 1999, including internal and external communication.
Strategy Review Committee	Chaired by an executive director.
Operations Committee	Chaired by an executive director.
Six committees at this level, include the Corporate Communications Committee	Chaired by an executive director.

In July 1998 Reuters announced that it was reorganizing its corporate structure, as of January 1, 1999, into two business divisions: Reuters Information and Reuters Trading Systems. Long standing geographical divisions were merged into a single distribution group responsible for the sale, installation, delivery, and support of the two divisions' products. The corporate relations department is classified as part of the information division with a direct reporting line to the finance director.

In a statement to staff, Chief Executive Peter Job said the reorganization was designed to achieve three main objectives:

- To increase value in the business by focusing on the profitability of business lines and their use of capital, with the aim of simplifying, speeding up, and economically managing the process of producing and marketing products.
- To exploit Reuters technology skills more actively to meet customer requirements to automate and improve their own processes.
- To focus top management more on the strategic evolution of the company, with less involvement in day-to-day matters and more opportunity for delegation of decision making to other managers (see Figure 9.1 for the organization of Reuters PLC as of July 1998).

Figure 9.1
Organization of Reuters PLC, July 1998

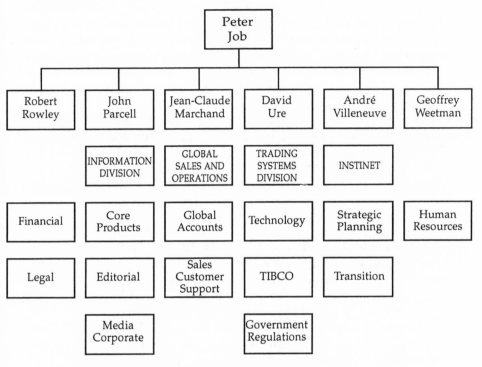

REUTERS HISTORY

In October 1851 Paul Julius Reuter, a German-born immigrant, opened an office in the city of London that transmitted stock market quotations between London and Paris using the new Calais–Dover cable. Two years earlier he had started to use pigeons to fly stock prices between Aachen and Brussels, a service that operated for a year until the gap in the telegraph link was closed.

Reuters soon extended his service to other European countries and expanded the content to include general and economic news. The reputation of his service was enhanced by a number of reporting scoops. In 1865 Reuter was ahead of any other agency in Europe with news of President Lincoln's assassination in the United States.

As telecommunications facilities developed, Reuters's business expanded to include the Far East in 1872 and Brazil in 1874. In 1883 the company began to use a "column printer" to transmit messages electrically to London newspapers, and in 1923 pioneered the use of radio to transmit news internationally. In 1927 it introduced the teleprinter to distribute news to London newspapers.

In 1925 the Press Association, the U.K. press agency, took a majority holding in Reuters and in 1939 the company moved its corporate headquarters to its present location at 85 Fleet Street. In 1941 the Reuter Trust was formed to safeguard the neutrality and independence of Reuters.

Reuters continued to modernize rapidly in the latter half of this century, with pioneering developments. The introduction of a succession of computerized products for international traders transformed the business, including the first international information retrieval system in 1964. The Stockmaster service, which transmitted financial data internationally, quickly proved a success and directed the company's focus toward computer services.

In 1973 a further innovative development was the launch of the Reuter Monitor, which created an electronic marketplace for foreign exchange. This service expanded rapidly to carry news and prices covering securities, commodities, and money and was further enhanced with the launch of the Reuter Monitor Dealing Service.

Following a dramatic increase in profitability since 1980, Reuters was floated as a public company in 1984 on the London Stock Exchange and on NASDAQ in the United States. On listing, the company had a market capitalization of some £700 million. Subsequently, Reuters made a series of acquisitions, including Visnews (1985) (renamed Reuters Television), Instinet (1986), and TIBCO (formerly Teknekron) and Quotron (both in 1994).

Reuters continued to grow rapidly, widening the range of its business products and expanding its global reporting network for media, financial, and economic services. Recent key product launches include Equities 2000 (1987), Dealing 2000-2 (1992), Business Briefing (1994), Reuters Financial Television (1994), and 3000 Series (1996) (see Figure 9.2 for a summary of Reuters milestones).

OBJECTIVES

Reuters Group PLC has three objectives:

- Reuters aims to grow its value for shareholders and outperform its peers. It will devote itself to the business of information and related systems technology, enabling professional communities to enhance their work performance in the fields of finance and commerce.
- Reuters's brand offers customers innovative use of well-supported technology, as well as swift and easy access to essential content, accurately compiled without bias. We will capitalize on Reuters's media businesses, which are profitable, to build our brand worldwide in newspapers, broadcasting, and on the Internet.

• The company aims to attract and retain good people through its unique international culture, the important values embodied in the Reuter Trust Principles, and the interesting opportunities it offers in terms of career development and participation in the success of the enterprise.

Figure 9.2
Reuters Milestones

1850 Paul Julius Reuter uses pigeons to fly stock prices between Aachen and Brussels.

1851 Reuter sets up his telegraphic agency in London using the new underwater cable between Dover and Calais.

1858 Offices spring up all over Europe, following Reuter's maxim, "Follow the cable."

1865 The Reuters report of the assassination of President Lincoln is the first to reach London, throwing European financial markets into turmoil.

1900 Mass celebrations in London on a Reuters report that British troops relieved the South African town of Mafeking, besieged by Boers.

1918 Reuters first with the news of Armistice that ended First World War.

1923 Reuters pioneers the use of radio to transmit news internationally.

1961 Reuters first with the news of the Berlin Wall being built.

1964 Reuters launches Stockmaster, the first use of computers for the international transmission of financial data.

1973 Reuters Monitor marks a world first with screen-based displays of real-time foreign exchange rates.

1981 The Reuters Monitor Dealing Service is launched, allowing dealers to make transactions on the Reuters network.

1989 Reuters first with the news of the fall of the Berlin Wall.

1992 Reuters pioneers electronic foreign exchange broking with the launch of Dealing 2000–2.

1994 Reuters Financial Television is launched, giving foreign exchange traders live coverage of market-moving events on their trading screens.

1996 Reuters launches the 3000 series of products, adding a huge new database of historical background information to real-time news and data.

REUTERS PRODUCTS

Reuters supplies information for professionals who use it to help them in their businesses. Financial market traders use the information to trade on markets, corporations use it to research markets and competitors, and the media uses it to create newspapers and television and radio programs. For the financial markets, Reuters also enables customers to make transactions over its worldwide private network. It gives them the means to distribute market information within their trading rooms or to outside offices, and provides computer software to analyze information before and after trading. Reuters divides its products into a number of different categories.

Information Products

This largest group of products is designed for financial markets. Besides real-time and historical information, it includes analytical software and information-management systems.

Information

The information Reuters provides to financial markets consists of financial data, obtained as feeds from exchanges or as direct contributions from clients, and specialized news about events affecting financial markets in more than twenty different languages.

Financial market traders have access to the same information at the same time wherever they are in the world. Global and national markets are made more transparent, and a greater number of traders can participate effectively. This benefits liquidity, and has been one factor in the big growth in financial markets over the last twenty years.

Customers can choose the geographical scope of the data and news they require, and the type of markets covered (e.g., money, securities, commodities, etc.). The information not only covers international markets such as foreign exchange, but increasingly also domestic markets for stocks, bonds, and other financial instruments in individual countries.

The information is received on stand-alone Reuters Terminals, or more frequently nowadays as datafeeds fed into clients' own in-house information-management systems. Besides textual news, Reuters provides live televised coverage of news that affects financial markets. Reuters Television allows traders in major markets worldwide to view live television with sound alongside data and news on their screens.

Reuters supplies information that is constantly updated in real time for traders who are constantly dealing in the markets. Customers also have access to a huge database of historical and background information, which enables managers of portfolio and investment funds to carry out pretrade analysis using computer programs. It includes data on more than 30,000 companies, economic indicators, market indices, and price histories of more than 100,000 equities and 350,000 bonds.

Introduction of the database led to the launch of the new 3000 series of products in mid-1996. This series combines historical information with real-time data, news, Financial Television, and a Reuters Mail e-mail service connecting customers and allowing them to transmit messages to each other. The 3000 series is one of the company's most strategically important new product packages in nearly a decade, reaching over 42,000 sales by the end of 1997.

Reuters supplies a wide range of decision-support software applications, designed differently for each group of users. The applications help decide trading strategies in advance, and also analyze risks resulting once positions are taken on various financial markets.

Demand for risk-management systems such as Reuters Kondor+ is growing strongly due to some well-publicized major trading losses and regulations requiring banks to measure risk more effectively. This is becoming an increasingly important part of Reuters's business.

Internet-Based Services

Reuters increasingly distributes information over banks' intranets (private internets confined to the bank), over Reuters Web (an extranet accessible only by Reuters customers), and the public Internet. These systems enable information to be circulated easily and cost effectively to users outside trading rooms, to bank staff working in retail and private banking, as well as direct to the banks' private investor clients.

Information-Management Systems

Reuters companies design and install information-management systems for banks' and brokerages' financial trading rooms. These enable all dealers in a trading room to simultaneously view information and analytical software, not just from Reuters but also from other vendors and their own internal information sources. The systems use advanced technology to circulate information over a network.

Reuters itself markets the Triarch product, while the wholly owned Reuters subsidiary TIBCO provides an alternative system using different technology based more on computer toolkits. Reuters and TIBCO operate independently and compete with each other, so customers have a genuine choice. Between them, Reuters and TIBCO are the largest suppliers to this market. These integrated trading rooms are frequently seen as backgrounds for business television programs. The underlying technology is now also increasingly used for distributing information beyond the trading room to banks' back offices and outlying branches.

Traders can also use digital voice dealing systems supplied by Reuters Voice Systems. Information products, including information-management systems, together account for 64 percent of Reuters revenue (£1,852 million in 1997).

Transaction Products

These are the products that allow traders to carry out transactions instantaneously worldwide over Reuters private network.

The most widely used Reuters transaction product is Dealing 2000-1, designed for the foreign-exchange market. A trader can establish contact with a counterpart anywhere in the world within two seconds, quote rates on a terminal screen, and confirm the deal. In 1992 Reuters introduced a foreign exchange electronic broking system, Dealing 2000-2. This automatically matches bids and offers put into the system by market participants, functioning as a broker. Traders do not have to hold an actual conversation with their counterparts. The Reuters subsidiary Instinet provides a similar electronic broking facility for traders in securities, which has seen dramatic growth in usage in recent years. It is largely used in the United States, but is also now established in Europe and the Far East. In Europe it operates in Switzerland, Germany, France, Sweden, and the United Kingdom. Transaction products account for 29 percent of revenue (£828 million in 1997).

Media Products

Media products are the original core of Reuters activities, based on well-established values of speed, accuracy, and freedom from bias. Originally they consisted of just textual news, but now also of still pictures, news graphics, and televised news film.

The flagship Reuters World Service of general news, published in English, French, German, and Spanish, is a comprehensive report of international news used by newspapers, broadcasters, and local news agencies worldwide.

Reuters launched the Reuters News Pictures Service in 1985 after acquiring the non–U.S photo business of United Press International. The Reuters News Graphics Service of computer-drawn graphics was launched in 1990.

Reuters Television News provides raw news film for television stations worldwide. A large proportion of foreign news film seen on daily television news programs comes from Reuters, which is a market leader in this field.

Reuters also operates a multimedia data network using the latest digital technology to transmit high quality video, images, and text.

Besides serving newspapers and broadcasters, Reuters is also a leading provider of foreign news for the emerging media reaching the home. It supplies news to a wide range of online services and Internet Web sites accessible to the general public. Media and professional products account for 7 percent of Reuters revenue (£202 million in 1997) (see Figure 9.3 for revenue by product group).

REUTERS SHARE HISTORY

Reuters was floated as a public company on the London Stock Exchange and NASDAQ in New York in June 1984, the first British company to conduct such a simultaneous flotation. The voting stock in Reuters had previously been owned by four newspaper associations, and Reuters came to the market with a complex formula of A shares held by those groups, who retained voting control, B shares offered to the public, and a single Founders share, which may be used to outvote all ordinary shares if other safeguards fail and there is an attempt to seize control of the company. "Control," for this purpose, means 30 percent of the shares. The formula was designed to preserve the independence and integrity of Reuters, which had since its founding built up—and zealously sought to maintain—a reputation for accuracy and freedom from bias in its reporting and other activities.

The A shares provision, however, initially deterred some major fund investors, and during 1989 Reuters reorganized its capital structure, resulting in the conversion of the A ordinary shares and B ordinary

Figure 9.3
Reuters Worldwide Revenue by Product Group, 1997

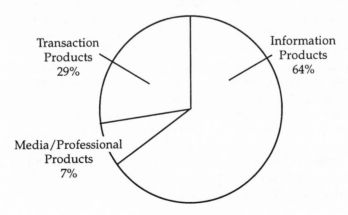

shares into one class of ordinary share. Chairman Sir Christopher Hogg said afterward, "The conversion of the A shares was a milestone for Reuters as a publicly-quoted company. It has undoubtedly led to wider interest in the company's shares."

In 1994, due to a rise in the share price over the preceding years, the 10-pence ordinary share was split in four to ordinary shares of 2.5 pence. The company has also carried out a number of share repurchases over the years. On December 4, 1997, the company announced its intention to implement a further capital reorganization, under which £1.5 billion ($2.475 billion) was returned to shareholders and Reuters Group PLC was formed to acquire the former Reuters Holdings PLC.

REUTERS INVESTOR RELATIONS PROGRAM

Reuters IR program is an integral part of its overall corporate, media, and external relations operation. It is headed by the director of corporate relations, Geoff Wicks. It is run by two teams, one in London and one in New York, with a further media and investor relations executive in Geneva. It was begun upon the advice of the investment bankers used to float the company. One of its key features is that it was started by, and continues to be run by, experienced people from within Reuters who know the company well, rather than bringing in people from the investor relations world. External advisors, however, are used extensively for advice and in monitoring the success of the program and the company's performance with major investors.

The key elements of the financial calendar are the quarterly figures. Since early 1994 the major half-yearly announcements—the preliminary and interim figures—have been broadcast live by video link between London and New York and always feature the chief executive and the finance director. As well as people in both audiences being able to see and ask them questions, there is an audio link where people unable to get to the venues can listen by telephone and call and ask questions. The slides used by the chief executive and finance director for their presentations are posted on the Internet so they can be viewed by people listening on the audio link. With Reuters having the facilities of its own television operation, these presentations are run as a full-scale outside broadcast (see Figure 9.4 for an organizational chart of Reuters PLC corporate relations).

Reuters was one of the first companies to pioneer such video conferences. For the Q1 and Q3 revenue statements there is a telephone conference. The Annual General Meeting is also treated as a major event, with the full board attending, as—even though usually poorly attended by institutions—it is an opportunity for the small shareholders to meet with the company in person and put their questions.

Figure 9.4
Organization of Reuters PLC Corporate Relations

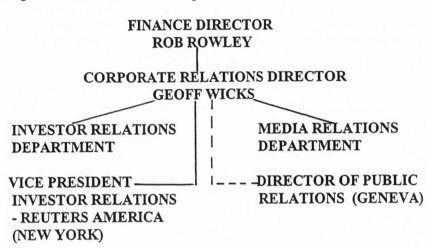

Reuters analyzes its shareholder register on a regular basis and targets its large holders for a visit once or twice a year by senior managers, usually the chief executive or finance director. The three senior investor relations executives in London, New York, and Geneva will also pay visits to key shareholders, see anyone who wants to talk to the company, and pay visits on a prospecting basis to people Reuters would like to have as shareholders. There are also people in the IR program available to talk to any and all shareholders, however small their holding, who want to call.

In addition to one-on-one visits, Reuters executives are regularly asked to speak at financial conferences and seminars. A shareholder magazine, *News from Reuters*, is mailed three to four times a year.

The investor relations department conducts an annual audit, in which investors and sell-side analysts are asked to rate the company on what it does well or not, what they would like changed, and whether the company's message is being put across sufficiently. The external advisers also independently monitor the people seen by the company, conducting confidential exit polls after major events, the interim and preliminary results presentations, and the visits by senior executives. The results of the audit and these surveys are presented in a report to the board once a year.

In December 1997 Reuters was named the most admired company in the United Kingdom by the respected monthly *Management Today*. The award is based on a survey in which Britain's ten largest companies in twenty-six sectors are asked to evaluate their peers against a series of criteria, such as quality of management, marketing, and goods and services. Calling Reuters, which finished sixth in 1996, "a worthy winner," *Management Today* said, "No one knows better the value of a good reputation than a news organization. Which makes the choice of Reuters Holdings as Britain's most admired company for 1997 all the more fitting" (*Management Today*, December 1997).

In 1997 Reuters was also named by the European Business Press Federation as one of the four finalists for its European company of the year award, *FX Week* magazine cited Reuters as the best electronic news service for the foreign-exchange industry, and the United Kingdom's *Investor Relations* magazine gave Reuters its 1997 award for best corporate governance. Announcing the award, based on a survey of U.K. analysts and fund managers, *Investor Relations* said, "Reuters has built up an implicit trust within the City (London's financial district), and trust is really the most essential part of corporate governance." In the same awards, Reuters was runner-up in the best investor relations officer category and best investor relations Web site section.

The Reuters Annual Report is taken very seriously by Chief Executive Peter Job and Finance Director Rob Rowley, who have a strong say in its design as well as its content. Since the company went public, the Annual Report has won numerous awards, both for its design and for financial disclosure. Since 1992 the Annual Report has featured a question and answer session with the chief executive, which has consistently been well received by investors and analysts both for the strong, topical questions as well as the detailed answers. "The Q&A section is an excellent idea, I'd like to see other companies doing it," one U.K. large fund manager said of the 1997 Annual Report.

In 1997 Reuters Annual Report for 1996 was ranked number one in an annual survey of Europe's top 500 companies by market capitalization by the Company Report *Report* publication. Commenting, the Company Report *Report* commends the chairman's statement for tackling the issue of a drop in the market value of Reuters shares during the year. "It provides a good example of the wisdom of tackling a problem rather than pretending it doesn't exist," it noted, adding, "He cannot resolve the issues in the space of the report, but what happens is that the reader is reassured that the company knows what the threat is, that it has the professionalism to respond to it, and that the shareholders' interests are regarded as paramount."

The Annual Report is seen as the window into the company for shareholders, customers, employees, and prospective investors. In 1997 Reuters was the first British company to put its full Annual Report on the Internet at the same time as the printed version was mailed to shareholders. The company Web site (www.reuters.com) contains information for investors among its many facets.

"Reuters have always disclosed very well. They are very up-front," one London fund manager said during a confidential survey undertaken by outside researchers after release of the 1997 Annual Report. "Reuters has integrity, as a company that knows where it is going. It is always looking to the future," added another large investor.

Since 1990 Reuters has staged a biennial Infoworld in Geneva to demonstrate products, make presentations, give briefings, and allow clients to meet senior members of management. At the 1998 Infoworld about 3,500 clients were flown in from around the world during its eleven-day staging, as well as about 100 people from the media for a press day and about fifty key investors for an investor relations day. One of them, Paul Eckley of State Farm, one the ten largest holders of Reuters stock, spoke to a management conference held to coincide with Infoworld. Eckley, State Farm's vice president for common stocks, said his company was a very long-term investor and one of its key criteria for selecting stocks was, "Does the Company have any concept of what an outside shareholder is?" Calling Reuters "very well managed," Eckley said,

I think Reuters does a very good job communicating with its shareholders. The Company is better at this than most all the firms we run across. There are two reasons why:

(a) Reuters is not a boastful organization. I appreciate this. Your results and strategy are communicated realistically and honestly. The comments you make are thoughtful and useful to me. I have always felt that I got a lot out of every meeting I have had with Reuters.

(b) I appreciate that the company makes a serious effort to inform investors every six months in good times, in OK times, and in tough times. Many organizations gather the analytical community together on a very occasional basis when they feel like it, or when they have something good to tell us. I always know that I will see you in another six months. That is very helpful.

With zero investors in the United States when it went public in 1984, Reuters had to build its U.S. investor relations program from scratch. The company also did not have any true peers to compare against, so it adopted Dow Jones, analyzed its holdings, and went after its institutional owners. Reuters senior management circled the country several times, giving presentations to every institution it could convince to come to a meeting. "It was a difficult and lengthy process," recalls former senior vice president of external relations. Michael J. Reilly, remembering how only two people showed up at a West Coast meeting and just four in Boston. The outcome, however, was positive, supported by consistent growth in revenues, earnings, and cash flow. Over a half dozen years, U.S. holdings grew to 49 percent.

But the 1990s did not match the dizzy share-price growth of the late 1980s. Delays and anticipation over new products and a market decline contributed to a sharp drop in Reuters's stock price. Over four years, U.S. holdings fell to about 30 percent of the company's shares and slipped further to about 24 percent in mid-1999. But, Reilly says, this chased away the "in and out" investors, who are more common in the United States than in Europe, and showed the wisdom of focusing on institutions whose investing styles center on finding companies they can hold over time. This represented a switch for Reuters, which had been following conventional IR wisdom at the time that suggested putting most of the effort into building the sell-side analyst "sales force." Now Reuters adopted two parallel strategies: building the most effective kind of sell side following, while stepping up contact and relationships with institutions.

The keys to an effective investor relations program, Reilly says, are consistency in communications, "staying with it, talking to people and treating them like human beings, responding to their calls, and seeing them regularly."

A major factor in Reuters's IR program is that, most unusually, major investors are also Reuters's clients. More than 53 percent of Reuters stock is held by only forty companies: asset-management companies, investment corporations, banks, and the like who do a great deal of their business using information and data from Reuters on equipment supplied by Reuters. Several of the company's biggest shareholders are also its biggest global clients.

"All publicly quoted companies need to understand their owners," says Corporate Relations Director Geoff Wicks.

Why do we put so much effort into our IR program? Because we want to focus more on shareholder value. We need to make sure they understand us, what we do, how we do it, our culture, aims, strategy and long-term ambitions so they can make a fair judgment about long-term prospects. We are in a broad and increasingly complex market. We are a global company with a global brand. As a result, we have strong shareholdings in many parts of the world and therefore have to run our IR program globally as well. Our goal is to have long-term stable shareholders who understand the business and work with us. We want to listen to their views and to be open with them so that we don't give the market any surprises.

Reuters prides itself on being very open and making a great deal of information available to shareholders, analysts, and others, often being the first to do so. In 1997 the monthly publication, *Company Reporting*, a semiofficial journal specializing in the review of U.K. annual reports, noted, "Reuters is the first company we have surveyed to disclose explicitly the establishment of a millennium program." The following year the same publication—which has the support of the accounting profession and standard setters in the United Kingdom—noted that Reuters was the first company to adopt a new standard of accounting for goodwill, FRS 10. Under a headline, "Reuters at the forefront (again)," *Company Reporting* said, "Reuters is the first company we have seen to adopt FRS 10 early." It added, "We are not surprised to see that this year, it is one of the first companies to discuss the cost of ensuring systems will be able to handle the introduction of the Euro."

The introduction of a single European currency, the Euro, on January 1, 1999, and the ramifications of the year-2000 computer-date problem posed major challenges to Reuters. To tackle them, two teams led by senior executives were set up and extensive documentation produced, both in published form and on the company Web site, to explain to shareholders, employees, suppliers, analysts, and others what the impact on Reuters would be and what the company was doing about it.

Wicks foresees greater shareholder activism in future investor relations activities. "Corporate governance is an increasing issue in the UK. There is pressure from the UK government for companies to do things in a certain way and for shareholders to have a greater say—pressure such as one-year contracts for directors, independent remuneration committees, increased shareholding voting on specific items such as salaries and directors' remuneration," he said. There is also the growing influence of ethical and environmental tracker funds. Wicks believes that awareness of shareholder concerns should be an integral part of the company culture at all levels. "To promote shareholder value, you need to get a shareholder perspective. Other people, not just senior management, need to know what shareholders are looking for," he says.

Wicks adds that the IR program plays a very important role in determining the day-to-day activities of the department.

There are a number of fixed events like results announcements and the AGM, a number of planned events in order for the company's senior management to talk to the larger shareholders in major centers and issues which arise on a frequent but unplanned basis that need to be handled. Our program for the whole year is mapped out as early as possible as getting time in the appropriate diaries is always a problem.

One issue that has been of concern to the investment community over the last year has been Y2K. Not only have we received many questionnaires from investing institutions checking on our readiness for the year 2000 but we are questioned in detail about the program and its costs at one on one and group meetings. In order to be as open as possible about the subject we organized seminars for investors in London and New York to discuss our Y2K program. This was of course only the starting point as the market also wanted to follow our progress and monitor the costs as the program moved forward. So we have a web site on which they can follow the progress and we give regular updates on costs in the half-year results statements. We have gone from Y2K being a concern to our investors who realized we had a significant task to complete, to having a prize-winning program. This has been achieved by consistently good communication.

There is increasing debate about the need to communicate with all shareholders equally, not giving large or favored investors any time or information advantage. With shareholders in many different time zones this is not easy, which is why for a number of years we have been giving results presentations simultaneously in both London and New York, as well as providing a telephone conference facility together with slides on the web for anyone who cannot be there. There is still a need to do more as private shareholders and the press want access to what have been essentially meetings for analysts. We will be able to provide much wider access via the web in the near future by setting up virtual conferences allowing anyone on the net to participate. The technology is available now but is as yet not widely available at the desktop of the users.

Looking to the future, Wicks notes,

Whilst we agree with the need to give equal access to all shareholders, this will inevitably change the level of communication. Analysts who have followed the company for some time and understand the products and markets in which the company deals will have the context for the information they are receiving. In future it will be necessary to give information at the lowest common denominator level, so that a private investor who has not previously looked at the stock will not be misled by any shorthand delivery of information.

10

Sony: The Story of a Unique Management Style and Financial Communications with Investors

Yoshiko Sato

Mr. Norio Ohga, former president of Sony Corporation, commented in the *Nikkei Financial Daily* of August 12, 1992, that he was unhappy about his company's share price, assuring investors that it was excessively discounted. He said that while Sony's book value per share (BPS) stood at 4,119 yen, its shares were traded at less than 4,000 yen. He emphasized that Sony had many promising projects which would generate greater cash flow. In addition, it had unrealized capital gains from stockholding. Since then, Sony's share price has more than doubled in six years. In July 1998 the share price reached an all-time high of 13,490 yen (see Figure 10.1).

For many years Sony's financial strategy has been quite different from many other large Japanese firms. Sony places an importance on capital markets as the primary source of its fundraising activity, while other companies have relied on banks for their financing needs. One of the possible reasons for this is that Sony has been aiming to be a globalized company. To be recognized in the foreign market, including the United States, it has tried not only to develop businesses but also to raise funds there.[1] Having engaged actively in overseas capital markets, Sony has learned the importance of disclosure and management-led investor relations. Forty-five percent of Sony's outstanding shares are held by foreign investors. An excellent relationship with current shareholders has attracted other foreign investors and contributed to its outstanding stock price.

Figure 10.1
Stock Price Movements of Sony Corporation

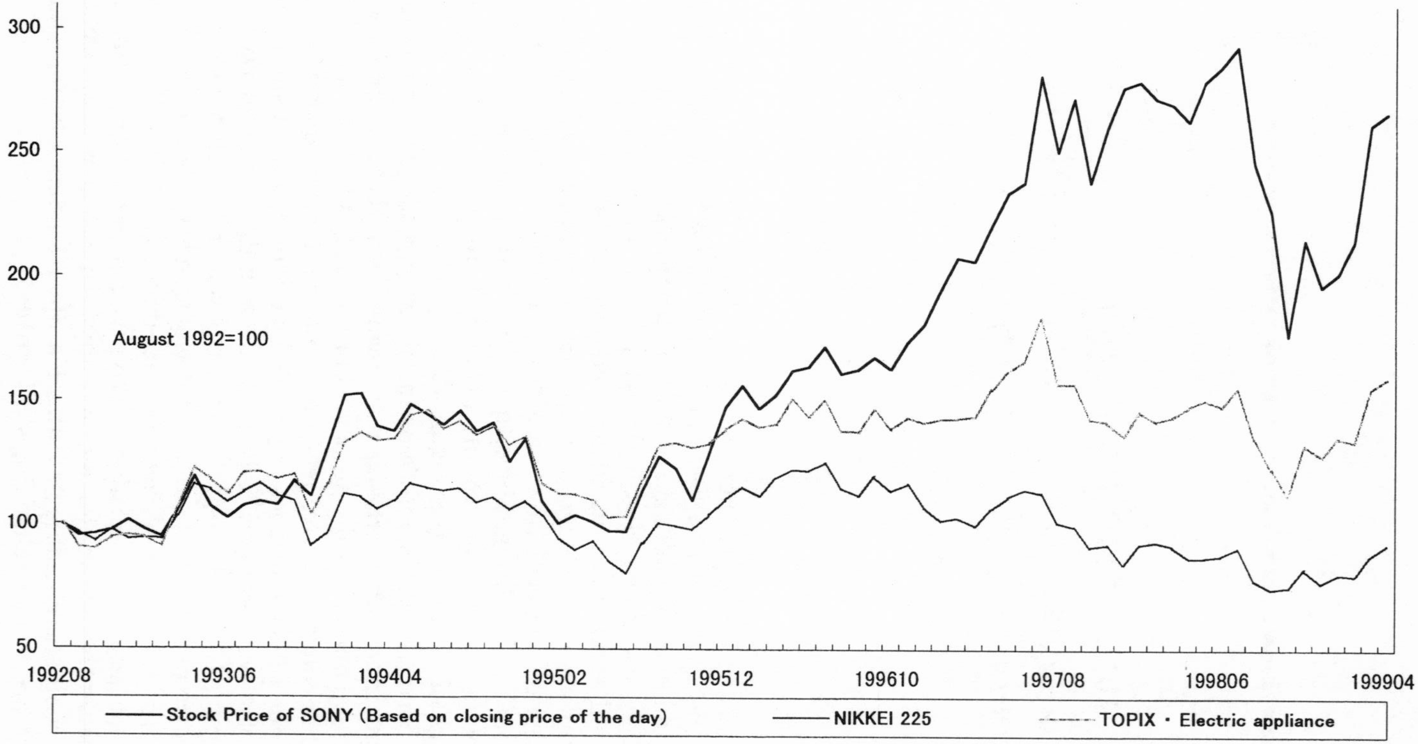
300
250
200
150
100
50
August 1992=100
199208
199306
199404
199502
199512
199610
199708
199806
199904
Stock Price of SONY (Based on closing price of the day)
NIKKEI 225
TOPIX · Electric appliance

One reason why Sony has an excellent relationship with investors is that the company's management understands the importance of communication. Many executives, including Mr. Akio Morita, one of the two founders of Sony, actively participated in the company's IR program. "The most important priority of an IR officer at Sony is to check Mr. Morita's schedule," said Mr. Sumio Sano, who was in charge of the company's financial communication when it listed its shares on the New York Stock Exchange in September 1970. As an indication of the importance that top management attaches to investor relations, Mr. Sano reported directly to Mr. Morita.

Timely and persistent disclosure has also won investors' support. Although most Japanese companies announce their business results twice a year, Sony reports consolidated quarterly results in accordance with SEC requirements. Soon after the announcements, its IR staff holds meetings and makes visits to analysts and investors to explain performance and strategy. These efforts are highly acclaimed by the worldwide investment community. As a result, Sony won the IR award from *Investor Relations Magazine* in the United Kingdom for the Asia–Pacific division in 1995 and 1996. In the United States, Sony won the same award in 1996, 1997, 1998, and 1999. Now Sony's IR philosophy is well recognized and highly regarded within the global investment community.

Sony has also developed a governance system that has helped to win the confidence of investors. Sony was one of the earliest Japanese companies to appoint outside directors to the board and reduce the term of directors to one year from two years. More recently, in 1997, Sony separated the decision-making and supervising function from the executive function, while these functions are still not clearly separated in most Japanese companies. One of the biggest public pension funds in the United States, California Public Employees Retirement Systems (CalPERS) applauded these steps and has commented that "other Japanese companies should follow."[2] It is an unusual move that such a fund with considerable influence on the corporate governance practices of many public firms should refer to a Japanese company.

While it has established an international presence, Sony maintains its Japanese identity. Mr. Nobuyuki Idei, president of Sony since 1995, has repeatedly emphasized the importance of its core business, manufacturing of electronic appliances. He continues to stress the productivity of the Japanese manufacturing system, which has been recognized as the highest level in the world. Despite its global presence, Sony is looking for ways to establish a delicate blend of U.S. and Japanese management styles.

Sony's IR department has been positioned between the market and the company itself. In other words, the IR staff plays a dual role, bridging between the market and the company by supplying information required by investors and feeding back views expressed by investors to the company. As internationalization progresses, management seeks greater capital efficiency. To achieve that objective, efforts are made by the IR staff to understand investors' viewpoints, while at the same time conveying the message to investors that the company is committed to the maximization of shareholder value. Sony's IR staff performs these tasks with the full support of its senior executives.

SONY'S INVESTOR RELATIONS

History of Sony IR Activities

What led Sony to start its active IR? The answer lies in the origin of the company that was established as a venture-capital company when such companies were rare in Japan (see Figure 10.2). When the Sony Corporation, originally called Tokyo Tsushin Kogyo Inc., was founded in 1946, it had some difficulties in raising funds because it was not tied with any company groups (*zaibatsu*) formed around a group bank. In addition, because other more established firms founded before the war had well-established domestic distribution networks from the early years, Sony saw more opportunities in foreign markets, especially in the United States. Aiming to be recognized in foreign markets, it tried not only to develop business, but also to establish local roots there. For that purpose, it was argued that the company needed to localize its operations, including its finances. Thus, apart from fundraising purposes, foreign stock listings have been an important tool for advancing the company's strategy to localize its operations globally, which is now called global localization.[3]

Sony's IR activities started with the introduction of an American Depository Receipt (ADR) program in 1960, at which time the company undertook an aggressive international marketing effort. The company's shares began listing on the NYSE in 1970 for the purpose of strengthening its fundraising capability, enhancing its multinational image, and developing a global management style. Adopting SEC rules, Sony appointed outside directors, reduced the term of directors to one year, and introduced quarterly earnings announcements. These measures became the basis for Sony's IR activities. Many foreign analysts and managers started to visit Sony, where they met with Mr. Morita and Mr. Sano.

At that time Japanese companies were not used to making presentations with comprehensive slides and pictures. Mr. Sano made efforts to improve their presentations by means of visual aids, such as charts, tables, and photographs of senior management. "If the photographs are in-

Figure 10.2
History of Funding and IR of Sony (Summary)

1946 May	Sony Founded
Oct	Initial Public Offering
1958 Aug.	Listed on the Tokyo Stock Exchange
1961 June	Issued American Depositary Receipt(ADR)
1970 Sep.	Listed on the New York Stock Exchange
	IR Department opened In New York Office
Oct	Listed on the London Stock Exchange
1975 Sep.	Obtained AA from S&P
1982 Feb.	Issued first private convertible bond
July	IR Department opened In London Office
1983 Feb.	Obtained AA+ Japan Bond Research Institute(JBRI)
1985 Oct.	Obtained A1 from Moody's
1992 Aug.	Started Information meeting for Individual Investors
1995 May	Started Information disclosure through the Internet
1996 Sep.	Filing 20–F through Electronic Data Gathering, Analysis and Retrieval(EDGAR) system as the first Japanese company

serted in the company's organizational chart, investors would be able to link the organization to the people," Mr. Sano explained. He made an effort to follow the annual schedule of Mr. Morita, and arranged for foreign investors to meet him as frequently as possible.

Mr. Sano was responsible for Sony's IR activities for twenty-five years, from when its shares were first listed on the NYSE until he retired to assume the presidency of Sony Precision Technology in 1997. He later recounted that not all the meetings with investors were uneventful. For example, when Mr. Sano was assigned to the New York office of Sony between 1974 and 1979, Sony's share price had dwindled to around $5 after heavy selling by foreigners. As this took place immediately after the oil crisis, many investors were anxious about the future of the company. Since the share ownership by foreign shareholders at that time had reached high levels, Sony needed to calm their anxiety. However, few fund managers were willing to meet with Mr. Sano, and the remaining few were very critical of Sony's future. Mr. Sano prepared a list of institutional investors, visited investors and analysts frequently, and asked analysts to send in their reports. These efforts eventually paid off when the number of Sony watchers increased.

Through numerous meetings with U.S. institutional investors, Mr. Sano learned the importance of forging relationships based on mutual understanding. Mr. Sano always accompanied sell-side analysts when visiting institutional investors, and asked for their opinion. Typical opinions and advice from analysts included comments such as "express your view, do not yield to what they say," and remember, "trust is easily lost by misleading investors." These meetings provided important experience when Sony expanded its IR activities.

During the 1970s Sony issued a series of corporate bonds. Since then, contacts with rating agencies such as S&P and Moody's have become an important responsibility for the IR staff. Through its discussions with the rating agencies, Sony soon realized who was responsible for determining Sony's share price. It recognized that not only the investment community, but also other parties' objective opinions might influence the evaluation of the company. Thus, Sony has maintained a policy of candid disclosure to the important intermediaries, including the rating agencies, ever since.

Meeting with rating agencies requires at least one annual presentation by the president of Sony. In 1975 there was an episode involving Mr. Morita when Sony was about to issue new bonds to finance a new factory for videotape recorders. Mr. Morita insisted that a videotape recorder be demonstrated at the meeting, emphasizing that creating innovative products is what Sony stands for. Usually, discussions with the rating agencies tend to be focused on numerical information. Analysts' reaction to the presentation by the president of the new product was quite favorable. Thus, a presentation by the president has become a part of meetings with rating agencies since then.

Another difficult moment arrived for Sony at its 1984 shareholders' meeting. Its Betamax-formatted VTR was about to lose its battle with the rival VHS format. Many shareholders demanded management accept responsibility for the failure. The annual shareholder meeting lasted more than thirteen hours, until 11:30 P.M., with endless questioning by shareholders. Mr. Ohga stood at the podium for thirteen hours and answered all the questions. He admitted that he was "tired" but that the "meeting was very useful, with many different opinions being exchanged."[4] The event was covered in the newspaper under the headline, "Doubt cast on confidence of Sony after losing its market share on VTR."[5]

Sony was also a target of the media when it bought the entertainment division of CBS for $2 billion in 1988, and later Columbia Pictures for $3.4 billion in 1989 from Coca-Cola. Despite hostile opinions from the media, the entertainment division has grown to become one of Sony's important revenue sources. In 1998 Sony agreed to pay a penalty of $1 million to the SEC to settle an alleged violation of accounting disclosure rules in connection with operations of its U.S. subsidiary. The alleged violations took place during the four months preceding Sony Corp of America's 1994 writeoff of approximately $2.7 billion of good will associated with its acquisition of Columbia Pictures Entertainment in 1989. The SEC claimed that since Sony began motion picture operations in the United States, the losses suffered by Sony Pictures were not discernible from its financial statements. Sony accepted the points raised by the SEC by adopting independent auditing for management's discussion and analysis section, appointing a CFO responsible for financial disclosure, and adopting the Financial Accounting Standard (FAS) 131 statement. Mr. Iba, deputy president, will become CFO and will assume responsibility for Annual Reports prepared by the capital market and investor relations department.[6]

Sony's Current Investor Relations Activities

Sony's IR activities that started with listing on the NYSE have expanded, targeting two major categories: institutional investors and individual investors. The most important activities are frequent meetings accompanied by sufficient information.

Presentation Meetings for Analysts and Institutional Investors

Mr. Masayoshi Morimoto, corporate vice president, usually represents Sony at major meetings. Over 200 meetings a year are held with institutional investors and analysts. Sony also holds quarterly meetings to announce business results every May, August, November, and February. In addition to these presentation meetings, visits to its factories and other company locations are prepared. Further, it holds small group discussions with analysts once a year, presented by executive officers and IR staff.

Sony was one of the first companies to undertake simultaneous teleconference calls connecting Japan, Europe, and the United States. These are conducted by Mr. Morimoto. It indicates that the company values fair disclosure on a timely basis. Furthermore, the IR staff visits more than fifty domestic and thirty overseas institutional investors to outline results of current operations. These various meetings are coordinated to match the needs of investors.

Annual Reports and Other Printed Matter

Sony prepared 113,000 Annual Reports (84,000 English and 29,000 in Japanese) as of 1998 for IR activities. Sony considers Annual Reports a tool for enhancing its corporate image, as well as providing information to shareholders. In its 1998 Annual Report, Mr. Idei sent a message that represents the company's vision:

The term "Digital Dream Kids" defines the future direction of new product development at Sony. This concept embodies our belief that Sony must continue to be a source of unique and enjoyable products that fulfill the dreams of our customers who are captivated by the potential of digital technologies. In addition, we have created the "Do you dream in Sony?" concept to convey the centripetal force of Sony and diverse business domains. This concept expresses the idea of making dreams come true at a place called Sony way, and along with the Sony family.[7]

Adding to this message, Sony states business strategies, including R&D, production, overseas developments, environment, and contribution to society, to illustrate its corporate strategy.

Consolidated financial statements are also prepared as a part of a proxy statement to shareholders. These statements have the same contents as the annual report, but are available three to four weeks after the announcement of annual results, aiming to provide information in a timely fashion. Form 20-F is one of the requirements of the SEC for non–U.S. companies. Reflecting a strong interest among U.S. investors, Sony has displayed 20-F information on the EDGAR electronic disclosure system since 1996.

Quarterly reports are distributed one week after the announcement of results. These reports contain information on new products, technology, and entertainment, in addition to the financial statements. Consolidated historical data are provided to analysts and investors who need to compare current results with past performance (see Figure 10.3).

Sony's printed materials, including fully consolidated statements, have three characteristics: simultaneously prepared in two languages, sufficient information on a consolidated basis, and timely disclosure that is released soon after the announcement. One of the reasons that the company does this is to comply with SEC standards. However, challenges still remain. Because it is difficult to convey the same content in English and Japanese, the company must pay attention to achieving clear expression in both the English and Japanese versions.

Other Investor Relations Activities

While Sony has been developing IR activities for institutional investors, it also devotes care to individual investors. Between 1992 and 1997 Sony held a series of presentation meetings at local branches of

Figure 10.3
Operating Income and Net Income of Sony

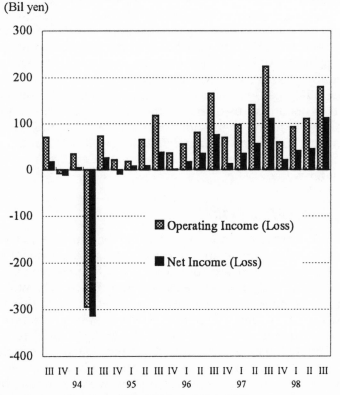

Source: Sony Corporation, *Consolidated Historical Data 1998*.

securities companies. The reason the company places an emphasis on individual investors is that its shareholders may also be important clients. Thus, presentations include a demonstration of its products in which individual attendees might be interested. Although it has ended this series, Sony spoke at the annual meeting of the Japan Association of Individual Investors in 1998 and held a presentation session for its investment club members.

How does the company treat the media? Sony holds presentations and organizes factory tours for the media every quarter. These tasks are shared between the public relations office and the capital market office. The company believes the media has a strong influence on the impressions individual investors have. The media itself also has an opportunity to use Sony's products. Utilizing the electronic media for swift distribution of its information, the company started using the Internet in 1995 for disclosure of annual and quarterly results. Information is also sent to analysts and institutional investors by fax. E-mail is now used for internal communication. Real-time share-price information is mailed to Sony's management in order to promote the value of IR in the company. One of the roles of the IR staff is to introduce investors' viewpoints within the company. IR personnel attend executive officers' meetings to report analysts' views. Recently they started to participate in the mid-term management planning council. Mr. Morimoto, who represents the IR staff, sometimes communicates to other staff in the company through the video news targeted for employees.

In summary, Sony's IR activities provide comprehensive disclosure based on SEC rules with which overseas investors are more familiar. Sony's IR is not unique by global capital-market standards, as the company is merely trying to provide what investors require. This, however, has put Sony in a very advantageous position among Japanese corporations, because few Japanese companies place a priority on shareholder value.

Organization of Sony's IR

Sony's IR is operated under Mr. Tamotsu Iba, chief financial officer, and by the capital market and investor relations department headed by Mr. Morimoto. There are approximately fifteen people working in the department, including overseas personnel based in New York and London (see Figure 10.4). There are other departments that interact with IR, such as finance, international accounting, and the corporate control department. This again shows the importance of IR at Sony, since not many Japanese companies have more than ten people in an IR department. According to JIRA research, only 5.1 percent of the respondents have an IR department, and its average number of staffs

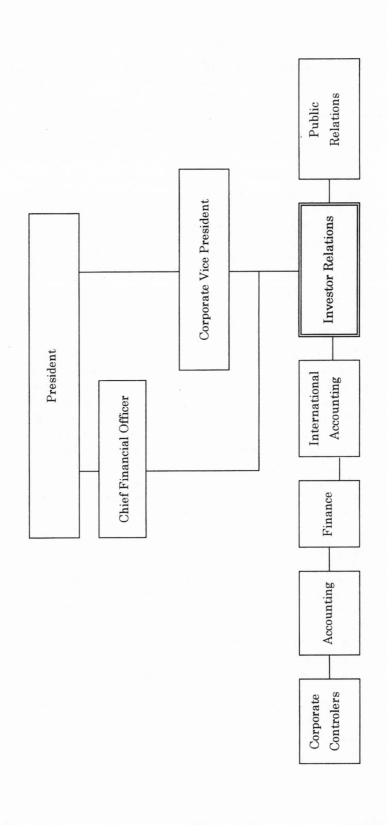

is 2.9.[8] Sony trains future IR personnel by giving them experience through assignments in finance, accounting, business promotion, and overseas offices. All current IR personnel have gone through these training programs and have became specialists in IR.

Sony's IR office started in 1970 within the president's office. As mentioned earlier, Sony's IR activity is synonymous with capital fundraising. Through fundraising activities, the linkage of top management and IR office was established at this early stage.

The involvement of the managing director who covers IR is another characteristic of its IR organization. Japanese directors often represent particular divisions of a company, but there are few directors who are responsible for IR or are chief financial officer like in U.S. companies. Mr. Sano, the former managing director, has worked hard as a representative of the company and the importance of IR has been understood and accepted by the top executives at Sony.

Involvement by Executives

Many companies have visited Sony to seek advice for their own IR. Mr. Sano used to tell them, "If your chief is not for the idea, don't do it." Mr. Sano was always confident that his activity had the full support of Mr. Morita. What makes an IR activity different is whether the chief is available and ready to answer questions when the company is in difficulty.

Sony's chief was always there, for example, at the time of the oil crisis and when Betamax was losing its share of the market. Sony's new chief may not be exposed sufficiently to investors, but Mr. Idei clearly expressed his vision for the company's future in the 1998 Annual Report, which includes the phrase "creator of dreams," and is expected to be more visible at future meetings.

Reputation in Investment Community

Sony has an excellent reputation in the investment community worldwide. It was the first winner of the excellent IR company prize awarded by the Japan Investor Relations Association in 1995. Reasons for this award include Sony's pioneering role in IR in Japan, commitment to timely and open disclosure, and readiness to answer investors' questions through its offices around the world.

Sony has also won top-level prizes for excellent companies on disclosure selected by research analysts by the Security Analysts Association of Japan. The company also won the first prize in the electronics field in 1995 and 1996. The prize is awarded based on total points for disclosure in the following areas: "business result reports and annual reports" (15 points); "disclosure at meetings, interviews and materials that are distributed there" (30 points); "timely disclosures, such as filing at the Tokyo Stock Exchange" (10 points); and "company information provided by voluntary disclosure" (15 points). It is also notable that Sony is a regular winner in the field of company information provided by voluntary disclosure.

Its reputation is also high overseas. As mentioned earlier, Sony won the Best IR Award in the Asia–Pacific division of the U.K. *Investor Relations Magazine* in 1995 and 1996, and in the United States in 1996, 1997, 1998, and 1999. The award is based on telephone voting by European and U.S. investors. Investors mentioned quarterly regular meetings, quick response by local IR representatives, and regular visits by top executives as reasons for voting for Sony. According to the investor community, Sony has excelled specifically in the following areas:

1. Long-term commitment.
2. Timely disclosure on a quarterly basis.
3. Responsive worldwide IR offices.

On the other hand, investors have requested more opportunities to meet with Sony's top executives.

INVOLVEMENT OF TOP MANAGEMENT

Review of the Management Structure

Sony began a major review of its management structure in 1994. After the introduction of the "Company System" in April 1994, Sony was restructured from nineteen business departments and eight divisions into eight newly created companies.[9] Substantial authority was delegated to these companies in order to promote faster decision making. Restructuring was accelerated when Mr. Idei was appointed as president of Sony. In March 1999 the company announced plans to realign and strengthen its group architecture. The objective of this change is to enhance shareholder value through what it calls "Value Creation Management."[10]

In 1997 Sony reorganized its board of directors and created a new management position called "corporate executive officer" in an effort to distinguish those individuals responsible for oversight from those responsible for management. Sony will make a further distinction by reviewing the current list of board members and reducing the number of individuals who also serve on the management committee.[11] Does this change affect its IR? According to Mr. Sonoda, an IR officer of Sony, one executive officer was said to have expressed his satisfaction in the improved efficiency.

Corporate Governance

In order to improve its system of checks and balances, Sony is poised to increase the number of outside directors. However, a requirement of Japanese corporate law necessitates that Sony maintain a board consisting of mostly inside directors. Sony's inside directors are also executive officers. A management committee, subordinated to the board and comprised of inside directors, determines the issues that will be further discussed by the board. Sony introduced the management committee in June 1997. The committee inherits the function of the former executive board, to plan and promote strategy at the executive level. A company operating committee was introduced in May after the restructuring of companies in January 1998. The purpose of this committee is to promote the independence of each company. After the introduction of group officers, executive officers at the same level in major affiliated companies are also appointed as group officers of equal status.

In order to establish corporate governance within the Sony corporate culture, consensus needs to be achieved among the employees. In that sense, a remuneration package that is linked to shareholder value will be the key to the success. A new remuneration package, linked to stock price, was introduced in February 1998 for senior managers and non-Japanese senior managers at overseas affiliates. Sony has been implementing a new value-based performance-measurement system that reflects the cost of capital for fiscal year 1999.

Faster Decision Making

Mr. Idei says, "Software applications run well on a strong operating system." He equates the Sony organization with software application and headquarters with an operating system. Each company is given substantial authority to facilitate quick decision making. To achieve this objective, Sony has established a company operating committee, which covers intercompany affairs. This attempt was made in the hope that each company will continue to achieve overall synergy while maintaining independence.

Global Business Strategy

The introduction of the Company System and subsequent restructuring in January 1998 had clear objectives: to enhance digital broadcasting and Internet-related business. Currently, half of Sony's revenue comes from audiovisual equipment, but Mr. Idei wants Sony to become a company that "fulfills the dream of its customers" by making information technology the core business.

In an announcement on March 9, 1999, Sony stated its divisional companies will be grouped into the three main business units (Home Network Company, Personal IT Network Company, and Core Technology and Network Company), and computer entertainment will be positioned as the fourth pillar of the electronic business (see Figure 10.5). Based on this strategy, which reflects the needs of the investment community, many analysts believe that "Sony will become a very efficient company which considers the cost of capital." On the other hand, some investors point out, "We cannot find which direction Sony is going." They say Sony places too much importance on the entertainment business, while its core business should be electronic appliances. For the IR department, narrowing the different perceptions between investors and the company will be more important as Sony continues to change. These comments were made in an interview (by the author) with several Japanese investors who wished to remain anonymous.

COMPETITION IN THE GLOBAL COMMUNICATIONS INDUSTRY AND THEMES FOR THE FUTURE

Management Style Maintains the Flavor of Japanese Culture

As the result of its strong global presence, 70 percent of Sony's profit comes from outside Japan (see Table 10.1). However, there is some discrepancy between Sony's image abroad and within Japan. Foreigners emphasize the foresight of management, which has led the company to become a very successful international company. Japanese regard Sony as a very innovative company with new products that many people could not imagine. Mr. Idei also emphasizes that the root of Sony is "manufacturing." In the 1998 Annual Report, he described Sony as a "complex" corporation with a broad domain. He said Sony must "continue to be a source of unique and enjoyable products that fulfill the dreams of our customers who are captivated by the potential of digital technology."

Its IR department has a role in helping investors understand this complexity. The company strives for both efficiency and a Japanese corporate culture. For example, when Sony implemented the executive officers system, Mr. Ohga wrote letters to the wives of executive officers who had not been appointed as directors, explaining that their husbands had not been "demoted." This continuing evidence of a paternalistic corporate culture assured no objection from executive officers. Efficiencies have been established over the years. One long-time employee of the company mentioned that Sony used to give awards to anyone who had perfect office attendance. Many diligent employees like him have contributed to Sony's numerous best-sellers.

Figure 10.5
Sony Group Organizational Overview

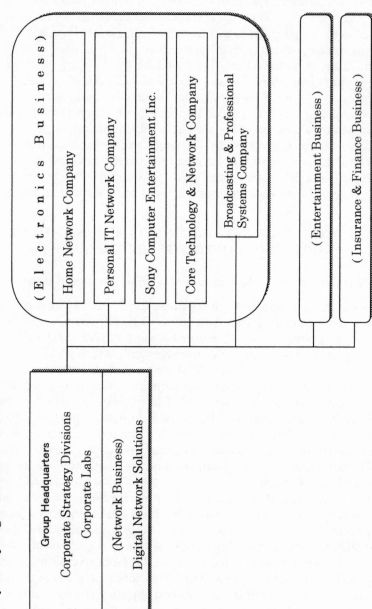

Table 10.1
Composition of Sales and Operating Revenue

	Fiscal year 1997		Fiscal year 1998	
	Mil yen	Composition (%)	Mil yen	Composition (%)
J a p a n	1,843,149	27.3	1,908,600	28.1
O v e r s e a s	4,912,341	72.7	4,886,019	71.9
U . S . A	2,101,907	31.1	2,157,061	31.8
E u r o p e	1,567,121	23.2	1,666,714	24.5
Other areas	1,243,313	18.4	1,062,244	15.6
T o t a l	6,755,490	100.0	6,794,619	100.0

Source: Sony Corporation, *Business Results,* 1998.

Further Issues Facing Sony's Investor Relations

Investors mention the following characteristics of Sony's IR program as positive and meaningful.

1. Commitment by top executives. Led by Mr. Morita, Sony's management has been supportive of IR efforts. Mr. Morita's ideas have been passed to younger generations of management. Commitment to the IR effort underlines the corporate activity in many fields.

2. Timely disclosure. Overseas investors appreciate the timeliness of disclosure. Sony's SEC-based disclosure succeeds in winning the confidence of many investors.

3. Clear objectives. Fundraising in the United States is the persisting objective of IR efforts. Sony supplies information to investors with this objective in mind.

4. Established corporate governance. The role of IR becomes clear when management is scrutinized by shareholders. Its efforts at restructuring have won the confidence of its shareholders.

5. Well-trained IR staff. Sony tries to maintain the competency level of IR personnel by established training programs. Efforts are made to provide the same response to investors' questions no matter who answers the inquiry.

On the other hand, investors want the following:

1. More involvement by top executives. Sony's senior management is committed to IR, but there should be more occasions for them to attend meetings.

2. More effort to go beyond SEC-required disclosures.

Investors understand the commitment of top executives, but they claim that Sony does not provide sufficient opportunities for them to meet with senior managers. They appreciate accurate and timely disclosure, but investors say that Sony's IR is not as innovative as it should be.

Furthermore, emphasis on shareholder value can interfere with the welfare of employees. An IR officer, while responsible for transmitting the advantages of maintaining a traditional Japanese management style to investors, is also responsible for conveying an investor's viewpoint to employees, including the importance of increasing shareholder value. Therefore, IR should explain why improving shareholder value will be to the benefit of other stakeholders in a comprehensive and logical way.

In summary, Sony's IR is highly acclaimed for its timeliness, accuracy, and fairness. Nevertheless, it sometimes fails to communicate the dynamics and uniqueness that Sony possesses. Sony must balance accurate and timely disclosure with a commitment to manufacturing, an investor's viewpoint, and the welfare of employees. The mission of Sony's IR is to balance these potentially opposing forces and to continue to impress the global financial community.

NOTES

1. Toru Yoshikawa, "Determinants of Investor Relations Strategy" (Ph.D. diss., York University, Toronto, Canada, 1997), 140–141.

2. *Nihon Keizai Shimbun*, 16 February 1998, 11.

3. Yoshikawa, "Determinants," 145.

4. *Nihon Keizai Shimbun*, 31 January 1984, 27.

5. *Nihon Keizai Shimbun*, 1 February 1984, 17.

6. Sony will not comment on this issue because of the terms of settlement with the SEC.

7. Sony Corporation, *1998 Annual Report*, 7.

8. Japan Investor Relations Association, *Survey of IR Activities in Japan*. Research report, March 1999.

9. The Company System is similar to the multidivisional structure employed by General Electric and many U.S. companies. At Sony, group headquarters oversee group operations, organize business units, and allocate resources under the concept of internal capital market.

10. Sony, press release, 9 March 1999.

11. Ibid.

11

Toyota Motor Corporation: Strategic and Financial Communications during Difficult Times

Yoshiko Sato and Toru Yoshikawa

The automobile industry is one of the most important industries in the economy, because such a large number of people, as well as companies in other industries, rely on it for their employment and businesses. As the leading company in this industry in Japan, Toyota has created many innovative products and developed new markets. However, the automobile industry is now facing the most difficult times in its history. It can no longer rely on the old system, which is based on the sales practice of using a large number of sales staff to make house calls and on the mass-production system developed over the past several decades. It needs to create and communicate a new strategic vision that reflects the various needs of a globalized society. A strong organizational capability that can enhance the company's product development, manufacturing, and sales is also required in order to survive in the global competition.

HISTORY OF TOYOTA MOTOR

Japan's largest automobile company officially originated from Sakichi Toyoda's company, Toyoda Automatic Loom Works Ltd., which was incorporated in 1926. An automobile division was first established within Toyoda Automatic Loom in 1933 with capital of 3 million yen (US$25,000 based on the current exchange rate of Y120 = US$1).[1] However, Kiichiro Toyoda, who was managing director of Toyoda Automatic Loom, had already been unofficially working on a project to design and produce automobiles before that time, although the domestic market for automobiles was still small in the early 1930s and dominated by General Motors and Ford.[2] As Kiichiro's project progressed, the project needed authorization by the company. Although Risaburo Toyoda, an adopted son of Sakichi and president of Toyoda Automatic Loom, was skeptical about the prospect of the automobile industry in Japan, he reluctantly consented to the plan. Thus, an automobile division was finally established in 1933.

At first Kiichiro had planned to produce passenger cars for the domestic market. However, he needed to start producing trucks instead of passenger cars in 1936 because of Japan's military operations in China and the economic recession in Japan. As Japan's military operations in China intensified, the Automobile Industry Act of 1936 was passed by the government, which designated Toyoda Automatic Loom as one of the two approved producers of cars and trucks (the other designated firm was Nissan). This provided Toyoda Automatic Loom a solid base on which to build its automobile business.

With paid-in capital of 9 million yen (US$75,000) and 3,123 employees, the automobile division became a separate company called the Toyota Motor Company in 1937.[3] The company's original stockholders were mostly family members, company executives, and Mitsui & Co.[4] This new company not only had significant capital, but it was also given a promise of support by large Japanese companies such as Toyoboseki, Mitsui Bank, and Itochu Trading Company.[5] Risaburo Toyoda was appointed as the company's first president because he was the head of the Toyoda family, and Kiichiro was elected executive vice president of the company.[6]

During the war Toyota prospered producing military vehicles, but it had a difficult time recovering after the war. The Occupation Forces first imposed a total production limit of 1,500 vehicles per month on the domestic automobile industry. Thus, in order to survive, highly trained engineers and factory workers of Toyota had to make everything from cooking pans to farming implements.[7] While the production limit on vehicles was finally lifted in 1949, another occupation policy, the so-called Dodge Line, was implemented.[8] The policy was designed to tighten up the economy to contain inflation. This policy led to an economic recession, which was not an environment conducive to passenger-car production.

In 1950 Toyota experienced a two-month labor strike, which halted the production operations of the company. In order to allow Toyota to sell vehicles, the marketing department was made an independent company with financial backing of a banking syndicate. This sales company was only merged with the production company in 1982. Toyota was facing a serious crisis at this time, and it was close to bankruptcy.[9] The company came under the control of the bank syndicate arranged by the Nagoya branch of the Bank of Japan and led by Mitsui Bank (then called Teikoku Bank), which sent its own executive, Fukio Nakagawa, to take on the position of managing director. The president of the company at that time, Kiichiro Toyoda, resigned in 1950, taking responsibility for poor postwar performance, and Taizo Ishida, president of Toyoda Automatic Loom, took over the presidency. The company came under the management of a non-Toyoda family member for the first time. However, Ishida publicly stated at the general shareholders' meeting that he would return the post of presidency to Kiichiro once the company recovered.[10] Thus, he suggested that management by a non-Toyoda family member would be only temporary.

As Kiichiro left Toyota, the Korean War started and the company was flooded with orders for military vehicles and other machines. This provided a great stimulus for Toyota to recover and grow. In the 1950s and 1960s Toyota undertook various innovations to improve productivity of labor, to reduce costs, to upgrade product quality, and to enhance management capability.[11] Some of the techniques that Toyota started to implement, such as the just-in-time system, later became benchmark practices of the industry. In 1950 Nissan was the industry leader with 54 percent of Japanese vehicle production as compared to Toyota's 29 percent.[12] By the 1970s, however, Toyota emerged as the largest automaker in Japan.

The company has continued to grow since the 1950s. In 1973 Toyota's sales were only slightly larger than Nissan's (the second largest automobile producer), at 1,355 versus 1,271 million yen (US$11,291,000 versus US$10,591,000).[13] But in 1987 Toyota's sales (4,307 million yen, US$35,891,000) were far larger than Nissan's (2,907 million yen, US$24,225,000). Toyota is now Japan's largest manufacturing company and the world's third largest automobile company. Hiroshi Okuda, president of the company since 1995 and a non-Toyoda family member, has been reportedly attempting to regain the share of the domestic market that the company has lost in the last few years.[14] Also, Toyota's decision-making process has been accelerated and its attitude toward shareholders has been improving, according to many observers (see Figure 11.1 for a recent ranking of production of automobiles in the world).[15]

NEW EMPHASIS AS A GLOBALIZED COMPANY

Compared with Toyota's 1997 Annual Report, there are some visible changes in its 1998 Annual Report. First, there is a new emphasis

Figure 11.1
Production Comparison by Automaker (Fifteen Selected Manufacturers, 1996, Including Overseas Production)

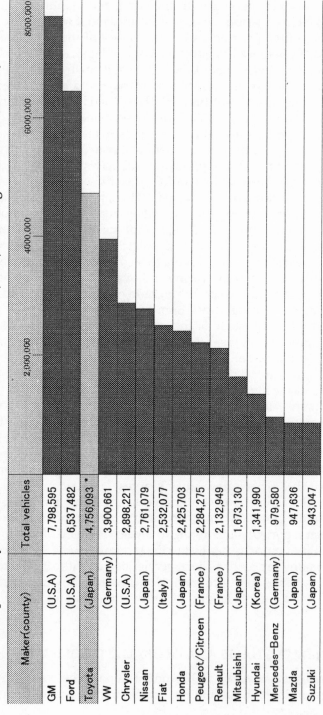

Maker(county)		Total vehicles
GM	(U.S.A)	7,798,595
Ford	(U.S.A)	6,537,482
Toyota	(Japan)	4,756,093 *
VW	(Germany)	3,900,661
Chrysler	(U.S.A)	2,898,221
Nissan	(Japan)	2,761,079
Fiat	(Italy)	2,532,077
Honda	(Japan)	2,425,703
Peugeot/Citroen	(France)	2,284,275
Renault	(France)	2,132,949
Mitsubishi	(Japan)	1,673,130
Hyundai	(Korea)	1,341,990
Mercedes–Benz	(Germany)	979,580
Mazda	(Japan)	947,636
Suzuki	(Japan)	943,047

Source: JAMA (Tokyo: Japan Automobile Makers Association, 1996).

*Toyota Motor Corporation official production figures.

in the message, "To Our Fellow Toyota Stakeholders," from top management of the company, including Shoichiro Toyoda (chairman), Iwao Isomura (vice chairman), and Hiroshi Okuda (president). "We maximize shareholder value over the long term by harmonizing the interests of all our stakeholders: customers, suppliers, employees, and members of the community at large, as well as shareholders. At the same time, we are stepping up our efforts to address the special expectations of shareholders."[16] This statement, which appears in the table of contents in the Annual Report, is highlighted to show that the company is committed to its vision. This is the first time that Toyota's top executives have used the word "shareholder value" in their public statements.

Second, there is a new emphasis in the company's strategy for the twenty-first century. Toyota is committed to the development of the ultimate eco car or environmentally friendly vehicle. In its first attempt to achieve this objective, Toyota launched a new type of automobile called Prius in 1997. It has hybrid energy systems that utilize both an internal combustion engine and an electric motor. In the special feature section in the 1998 Annual Report, the development story of this new vehicle and the strategy for the future are presented.

Third, a "Review of Operations" is included in the Annual report. In addition to the review of the state of its operations in Japan and global markets, Toyota's production system, diversified operations, and financial policy are featured in the Annual Report. Toyota's ability to earn large profits based on its efficient mass-production systems has been recognized worldwide. However, some critics argue that such systems do not match today's consumer-oriented market. To this criticism, Toyota has responded as follows: "The future of the Toyota Production System lies in renewed flexibility. We are increasing flexibility at large plants in industrialized nations by equipping them with multipurpose equipment. And we also are achieving unprecedented flexibility at small plants in emerging economies." In the section on financial policy in the Annual Report, the company emphasizes the strength of its balance sheet based on two indicators: equity to asset ratio at 43.5 percent and 2.7 trillion yen of liquid assets (cash and cash equivalents plus short-and long-term investments in related businesses).[17]

Last, the environmental report was newly issued. In December 1998 Toyota introduced a 109-page report that contains Toyota's various environmental initiatives in each of its value-chain activities.[18] The issuance of this report by Toyota was motivated by the recent moves of some progressive automobile manufacturers such as GM, Daimler-Benz, and Volvo. These companies have released environmental reports because of their accountability to the community, and because how companies deal with environmental issues will be closely watched by the investment community. Toyota established the environmental affairs division, headed by President Hiroshi Okuda, in December 1998 and prepared for the issue of this report.

CHANGING MARKET CONDITIONS FOR THE AUTOMOBILE INDUSTRY

For a long time, Japanese automobile manufacturers have maintained their leading position in the world market. However, the radical changes in this industry and its environments have forced them to develop a new strategy to survive in the world market. The most visible issue that has significantly affected Japanese automobile companies has been the Asian crisis in 1997. According to the Japan Automobile Industry Association, the total units of export to Asia in fiscal year 1997 was 532,769, down 87.9 percent from the previous year. Further decline is expected for fiscal year 1998, and some analysts predict that the situation will not recover until the next century. Thus, Japanese automobile manufacturers may continue to suffer from the poor market conditions in the region for some time. A continued sluggish economy in the domestic market is the major problem. Because of the decline in individual consumption and capital investment, the Japanese economy is expected to record negative growth in fiscal 1998. In the automobile industry, the sales units of vehicles in fiscal 1998 will decrease to 5,879,000, 93.5 percent of the previous year.[19] Because of the difficult conditions, Japanese auto manufacturers are under pressure to initiate a radical restructuring to recover their sales in Japan.

As mega-mergers in the world market become common, more and more large auto manufacturers are going to find their partners beyond national borders, as in the cases of Daimler-Chrysler and Renault-Nissan. To survive in the competitive market, Japanese auto manufacturers need to express their strategic vision and develop a world-class disclosure and communications policy. One of the most important issues for the world automobile industry is how auto manufacturers deal with environmental problems. If the companies cannot introduce appropriate measures, the investment community may assume that there will be intangible risks. Some leading auto manufacturers, such as GM, Volkswagen, and Daimler-Chrysler, already started to release their environmental reports a few years ago. Japanese auto manufacturers need to move quickly in this area. Although capital investment and research and development for these purposes are significant, auto manufacturers have no choice but to make large investments. Although it is not easy to estimate costs required to resolve the environmental problems in the future, the investment community is waiting for clear information and actions from auto manufacturers.

TOYOTA'S IR ACTIVITIES

Corporate Finance and IR Activities

While Toyota relied on bank borrowings from the establishment of the company until the 1960s, its financing strategy shifted from bank loans to internal cash and capital-market financing quite early. When the company was founded in 1937, Mitsui Bank was one of the financial supporters.[20] In 1950, when the labor strike started, Toyota was put under the control of a bank syndicate led by Mitsui Bank, which also sent its own executive, Fukio Nakagawa, to the company's board. The company was given financial support from banks on the conditions that it be separated into sales and production companies and that Kiichiro resign as president. From the late 1940s to the early 1950s, because of financial difficulties, Toyota's relations with Mitsui Bank strengthened, although the Toyoda family's ties with the bank dated back to World War I.[21]

However, Toyota has substantially reduced its financial reliance on banks since then, especially since the mid-1960s. By 1977 the company had no bank borrowings on an unconsolidated basis.[22] Since that time, Toyota's financing needs have been met by internal cash and, increasingly in the 1980s, by capital-market financing. In fact, because of its high internal cash position, the company is referred to as the "Toyota Bank" in Japan.[23]

Today, as the company's sales in foreign markets increase, Toyota uses capital markets extensively in Japan and in foreign countries through its finance subsidiaries. Such subsidiaries include Toyota Motor Credit Corporation, established in 1982 in the United States, Toyota Finance Australia Ltd. (1982), Toyota Motor Finance (Netherlands) B.V. (1987), and Toyota Credit Canada (1990).[24] These subsidiaries raise a larger amount of debt capital from the markets than their parent. For example, outstanding long-term capital-market debts of the parent company were 531,740 million yen (US$$4,431 million) as of March 1996, while those of consolidated subsidiaries were 1,422,138 million yen (US$11,851 million). They use these market funds to support automobile sales in local markets through car loans and car leasing. Thus, as automobile sales increase in foreign markets, fundraising activities by these subsidiaries also increase.

Because of the growing amount of capital-market financing due to rising foreign sales, Toyota has been conducting IR activities in foreign markets through road shows, which are mainly targeted at institutional debt investors. In addition to debt financing, Toyota listed its shares on the New York Stock Exchange in September 1999. These moves reflect the company's need to finance its local operations in the

U.S. market and its desire to be recognized as a globalized company that follows international rules. Thus, Toyota now has a strong incentive to enhance its IR activities, especially toward overseas investors who provide capital to Toyota's foreign operations.

History of Toyota's IR Activities

Japanese disclosure rules are often viewed as less stringent that those based on SEC standards. Although Toyota's American Depositary Receipt has been listed on the NASDAQ system since 1971, the company has not been following SEC disclosure standards because it is exempted from the requirements (firms are legally exempt from the use of the SEC standards if securities are privately placed or the issue amount is smaller than US$1.5 million). Among Japanese automobiles, Honda is the only company that discloses information based on SEC standards. Therefore, compared to other internationally oriented Japanese firms such as Honda and Sony, Toyota so far has not been emphasizing information disclosure.

Toyota started to hold investor meetings in foreign locations in 1983, but it was during the bubble economy period in the late 1980s when the company began to hold overseas meetings more frequently, especially in Europe, in order to promote its new Eurobond issues. In these meetings, the executive vice president or managing director was usually present to explain the company's financial position and performance. For equity investors, however, Toyota has not been engaged in active IR activities. This lack of interest can be explained, in part, by Toyota's ownership structure, in which foreign investors held only 1.8 percent of its outstanding shares in 1989. In addition, a large portion of Toyota's shares had been held by stable shareholders, including its *keiretsu* firms and friendly financial institutions. Because of this ownership structure, Toyota did not devote much attention in its IR activities to equity investors. However, there are some signs that this attitude is gradually changing because of the changing market environments as discussed in the earlier section.

Major Characteristics

Toyota's IR activities have three characteristics: no independent IR department, few opportunities for analysts and investors to meet the president directly, and equal treatment between shareholders and other stakeholders despite the company's new emphasis on shareholder value.

At Toyota, four divisions are involved with IR activities: accounting, finance, general affairs, and public affairs (see Figure 11.2). Although its headquarters are located in the city of Toyoda, the company

Figure 11.2
IR Organization of Toyota

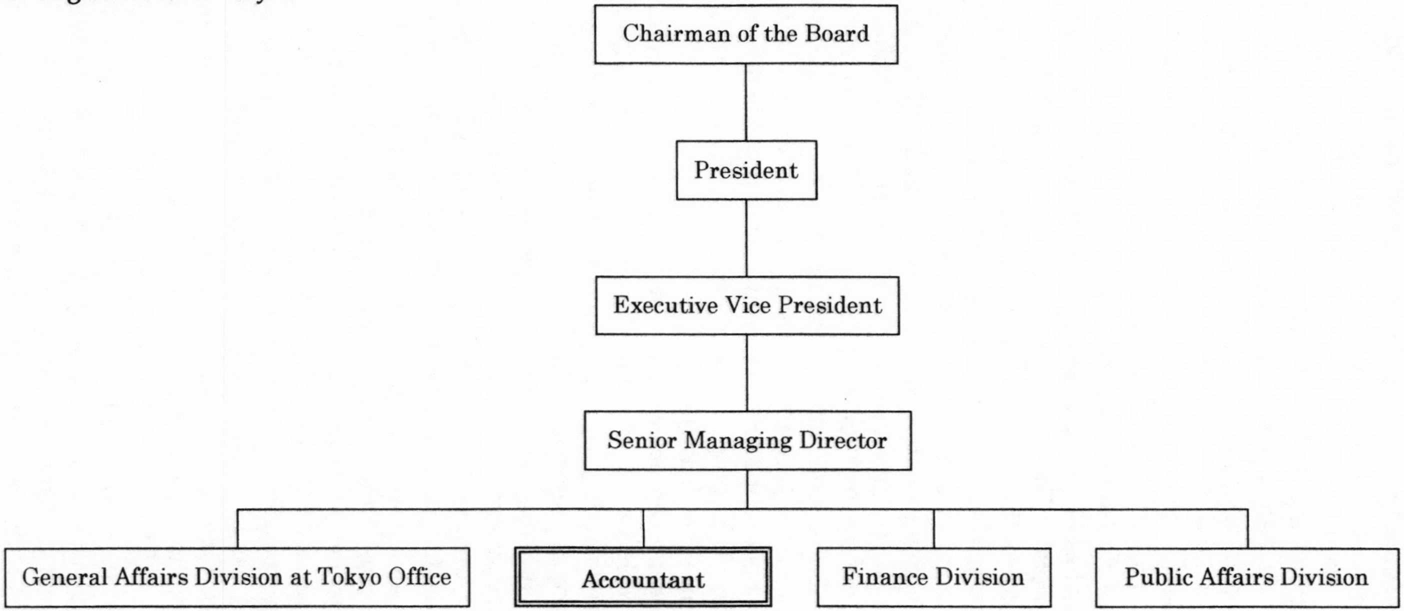

also has some IR personnel in the general affairs and public affairs divisions in its Tokyo office. "We see the accounting division as the center of the IR related activities," Takeshi Suzuki, general manager of the accounting division stated at the seminar in July 1998 for Japan Investor Relations Association members. Mr. Suzuki explained the advantage of not having an independent IR department at that seminar as follows: "If the company establishes an independent department, staff in other divisions might be reluctant to provide information. For example, detailed information on capital investment, which might provide a clue to its competitors as to what kind of new projects the company has been engaged in, would be difficult for the IR department to obtain. The accounting department is able to gather such internal information more smoothly. You can contact other departments more easily when you need further information." Shin Kanada, general manager of public affairs in Tokyo, adds, "We might be able to have a meaningful discussion if we establish the IR department. However, we should disclose information first to the public. This is because some information may be sometimes very sensitive in nature and therefore a disclosure of such information to only analysts or large investors may be construed as the violation of the insider trading regulations. I believe the first step would be to provide the information to the media. The company should think of IR as one of the corporate communications activities."[25]

The second characteristic of Toyota's IR activities is the way President Hiroshi Okuda becomes involved with such activities. He has been known as the "top management whose face can be seen" since he took office as president in 1995. In fact, he has actively been expressing his views on various issues to the mass media. His decision making is also recognized as quick and clear within Japanese industrial circles. "Compared to 10 years ago, the speed of change is now three times as fast. You do not have to think too deeply before you act. Speed and knowledge are the key to win the competition. I do everything as fast as I can," Okuda stressed in an interview in March 1999.[26] Some people believe that one of the reasons he can make decisions quickly is that he is not a member of the Toyoda family. For a long time, Toyota has been recognized as a company with a conservative corporate culture that has been established through the management by family members. Okuda is Toyota's first president not from the family in twenty-eight years in a company that was established by Kiichiro Toyoda in 1933. He is very outspoken and often considered an individual who can break the company's conservative culture.

In April 1998 Toyota's top management, including Okuda, set up a small meeting with analysts. Before that, top management had been hardly visible at IR activities. Although this new attempt was very much appreciated, Mr. Okuda has not appeared in front of the investment community since. Regarding this change, Takashi Hida, assistant manager of the accounting department stated, "Okuda already has a lot of opportunities to express his ideas through the mass media. In order to ensure the equal opportunity for every analyst and investor to hear his opinions and views, we are not going to have information meetings between Okuda and a limited number of analysts at this moment."[27]

At the information meeting to report year-end results, Managing Director Ryuji Araki, who is responsible for accounting and finance, mainly answers questions from analysts now. From the corporate communications side, Director Takashi Kamio gets involved with the IR activities, depending upon the issues and circumstances. Toyota has established its own style of IR activities, characterized by the division of tasks between the president, who expresses his views mainly through the media, and other executives, who are the main direct contacts with the investment community.

The third characteristic of Toyota's IR activities is that they try to balance the interests of shareholders and other stakeholders. Toyota has about 70,000 employees and many customers and suppliers. In the 1998 Annual Report it promised to pursue the maximization of shareholder value. However, this was mentioned in the section, "To Our Fellow Toyota Stakeholders," and it is stated that its goal will be achieved by "harmonizing the interests of all our stakeholders."[28] Compared to this, many U.S. companies start their annual reports with "Dear Fellow Shareowners" or "Letter to Shareholders." It is apparent, as is clear from the following statement, that Toyota uses an approach that considers the interests of all the stakeholders, not only of shareholders. "We create shareholder value by improving our customer satisfaction. As a going concern, a company should not focus their interest on a specified stakeholder," Kanada said, emphasizing this view of the company.

Evaluation in the Investment Community

In October 1998 Toyota was commended as one of the IR excellent companies by JIRA. The evaluation committee praised Toyota by stating that "the speech and behavior of top management are highly evaluated as one of the representative Japanese international companies in terms of IR activities. Business segmented information on a consolidated basis is very thorough and the quality of materials being provided at the information meeting is also high" (press release by the Japan Investor Relations Association, November 1998).

Table 11.1 shows the results of the evaluation of Toyota's IR by ten independent reviewers.[29] The farthest right column indicates the per-

Table 11.1
Evaluation of the IR Activities of Toyota Motor Corporation

	A	B	C	D	E	F	G	H	I	J	Average	Average/TopGrade
Clear Objectives	4	3	5	5	4	7	5	5	4	5	4.7	67.14%
IR Organization	9	7	10	9	8	11	6	10	6	9	8.5	60.71%
Top Management	8	6	9	10	9	12	8	7	3	7	7.9	56.40%
Disclosure	23	15	25	29	21	22	23	23	14	24	21.9	62.60%
Feedback	4	3	5	7	5	5	4	5	2	4	4.4	62.90%
IR Staff	18	12	19	28	19	24	107	19	14	18	27.8	99.20%
Tools & Events	14	12	13	16	12	21	13	11	11	15	13.8	65.70%

Source: A research report by the Japan Investor Relations Association (Tokyo: JIRA, 1998).

centage received out of the top grade. Toyota exceeded the average points in each category, and the quality of its IR staff received especially high marks.

In another survey of the disclosure practices by the Security Analysts Association of Japan, Toyota got the third position in the automobile industry in 1998. In that survey, Honda was selected as the best for its disclosure practices and Mitsubishi Motors was chosen as the most improved company. The evaluation committee stated that "Honda's top management is leading IR activities. For example, top executives themselves explain management policy and attend meetings to exchange ideas with analysts on the company's research and development policy. Quarterly disclosure is also appreciated" (Evaluation Committee of the Security Analysts Association of Japan, "A Survey of Disclosure Practices in Japan"; this comment was made in an interview by the author in October 1998). These two different results indicate that Toyota's IR strategy has succeeded in one way. Its improved attitude toward fair disclosure policy has been appreciated, although some analysts are still frustrated with the lack of direct contact with top management.

Noriyuki Matsushima, senior analyst at Nikko Salomon Smith Barney, stated, "I believe that Hiroshi Okuda's decision making is very quick and focused. Toyota's attitude toward information disclosure has been very much improved since Okuda became President. The problem is that since the IR related divisions work separately, I cannot believe that they have frequent contacts with each other."[30] This suggests that Toyota's IR practices are not well coordinated.

STRATEGY FOR THE FUTURE AND MESSAGE TO INVESTORS

It is difficult to predict how business conditions surrounding the automobile industry are going to evolve. Each company is under pressure to show their strengths to survive the market competition. Toyota is no exception. Some senior analysts argue that the company needs to restructure the sales system and cut labor costs. The old type of marketing system, which uses five distribution channels and frequent visits to its customers, might not be accepted by new types of consumers. Younger consumers prefer to choose cars by themselves at the showrooms rather than listening to aggressive recommendations by salespeople. How Toyota restructures the sales system in the domestic market will be the key factor in evaluating the company's investment prospects, according to one analyst.

As for performance targets, Toyota has not released any numerical targets, such as ROE. At small meetings with analysts, it provides a

Figure 11.3
Stock Price Movements of Toyota Motor Corporation

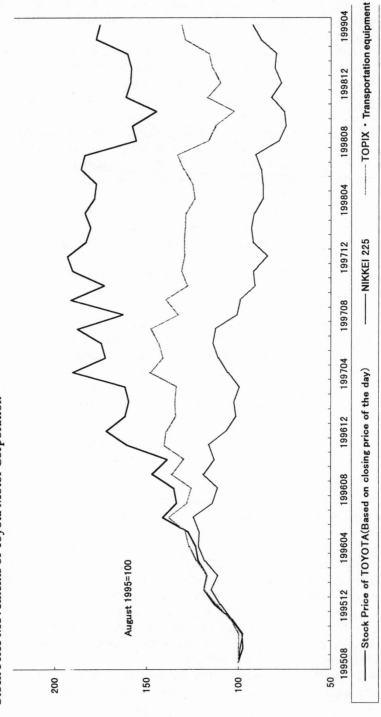

August 1995=100

─── Stock Price of TOYOTA(Based on closing price of the day)   ─── NIKKEI 225   ······· TOPIX · Transportation equipment

target range by saying, "We aim for the level of ROE of 10 percent," without indicating specific figures. Causes of change in operational profit, how the company manages to cut cost effectively, management policy for the future—these are the topics at the meetings. "Nobody knows who will be a winner. All we can do is to make our best efforts," said Shin Kanada, general manager of the corporate communications department.[31]

Why do many investors support this attitude of Toyota? Its stock price remains in the higher range among the Japanese auto manufacturers (see Figure 11.3). One of the reasons is its healthy financial position. "Since it is a cash-rich company, Toyota can take sufficient time to build an effective strategy. Other companies, which cannot afford to, need to hammer out the powerful strategy quickly to survive the market," according to Senior Analyst Matsushima.[32]

In 1998 Toyota made the top ranking in terms of EVA (Economic Value Added) and MVA (Market Value Added) among Japanese companies in a survey by the Japan Economic Journal and Stern Stuart, a U.S. consulting firm.[33] This result strongly suggests that Toyota has employed its capital efficiently and improved its profitability. In the investment community, many analysts recommend Toyota as "buy" for mid- to long-term investment. Despite its stellar performance, however, these analysts also hope to see more specific performance targets. How will Toyota communicate an attractive strategy that enhances the interests of all stakeholders? The market is looking forward to hearing the answer.

NOTES

1. K. Odaka, K. Ono, and F. Adachi, *The Automobile Industry in Japan: A Study of Ancillary Development* (Tokyo: Kinokuniya, 1988).

2. M. Cusumano, *The Japanese Automobile Industry: Technology and Management at Nissan and Toyota* (Cambridge: Harvard University Press, 1985).

3. Odaka, Ono, and Adachi, *Automobile Industry.*

4. Y. Togo and W. Wartman, *Against All Odds: The Story of Toyota Motor Corporation and the Family That Created It* (New York: St. Martin's Press, 1993).

5. K. Kajiwara and T. Takagi, *Hikaku Nihon no Kaisha: Jidousha* (Comparison of Japanese Companies: Automobile) (Tokyo: Jitsumu Kyoiku Shuppan, 1996).

6. Togo and Wartman, *Against All Odds.*

7. W. M. Fruin, *The Japanese Enterprise System: Competitive Strategy and Cooperative Structures* (Oxford: Clarendon Press, 1992).

8. Economic policy to control hyperinflation was recommended by a Detroit banker, J. M. Dodge. He called for a balanced budget, elimination of government subsidies to industries, and initiation of a fixed exchange rate at 360 yen per US$1.

9. Odaka, Ono, and Adachi, *Automobile Industry*.

10. Kajiwara and Takagi, *Hikaku Nihon no Kaisha*.

11. Fruin, *Japanese Enterprise System*.

12. Cusumano, *Japanese Automobile Industry*, 98.

13. Fruin, *Japanese Enterprise System*.

14. Kenyi Nagano, "The Challenge of Toyota," *Nikkei Business*, 26 August 1996, 33–37.

15. Toyota announced in April 1999 that Chairman Shoichiro Toyoda will be made honorary chairman, while President Hiroshi Okuda will take over as chairman. Vice Chairman Iwao Isomura will remain in his post and Executive Vice President Fujio Cho will become president after the board meeting following the company's annual shareholders meeting in June 1999.

16. Toyota Motor Corporation, *1998 Annual Report*, 3.

17. Ibid., 20.

18. Toyota Motor Corporation, *Toyota Environmental Report 1998*.

19. Japan Automobile Association, 19 March 1999 (Data obtained from the Web site of the Japan Automobile Association).

20. Kajiwara and Takagi, *Hikaku Nihon no Kaisha*.

21. Cusumano, *Japanese Automobile Industry*, 98.

22. Ibid.

23. J. Abegglen and G. Stalk, *Kaisha: The Japanese Corporation* (New York: Basic Books, 1985).

24. Toyota Motor Corporation, *The Automotive Industry: Toyota and Japan* (Tokyo, Japan: Toyota Motor Corp., International Public Affairs Division, 1996).

25. Shin Kanada, general manager of public affairs in Tokyo, interview by Yoshiko Sato, Tokyo, Japan, 10 August 1998.

26. Akio Irenka, "Management Innovation with Rapid Pace," *Wedge* (March 1999): 56–58.

27. Takashi Hida, assistant manager of the accounting department, interview by Yoshiko Sato, Tokyo, Japan, 2 April 1998.

28. Toyota Motor Corporation, *1998 Annual Report*, 2.

29. At the examination, ten independent reviewers representing different research teams graded two to six questions in seven categories. Total points compiled and results from a former screening process decided the "IR excellent" companies.

30. Noriyuki Matsushima, senior analyst of Nikko Salomon Smith Barney, interview by Yoshiko Sato, Tokyo, Japan, 16 April 1998.

31. Ibid.

32. Ibid.

33. *Nihon Keizai Shimbun* (Japan Economic Journal), 18 March 1999.

PART **III**

LESSONS TO BE LEARNED FROM LEADING GLOBAL STRATEGIC AND FINANCIAL COMMUNICATIONS COMPANIES

12

Key Success Factors in Global Strategic and Financial Communications

Before looking at lessons to be learned from leading strategic and financial communications companies, the following is a collage of fleeting, fragmentary, and largely random impressions drawn from Part II of the book:

- The "Digital Dream Kids," defining the future direction of new product development at Sony—Emphasizing the importance of communicating a compelling strategic vision to various stakeholders.

- The "Reuters Trust Principles"—Highlighting the bedrock values of corporate credibility based on independence and integrity.

- "Maximizing shareholder value over the long term, harmonizing the interests of all Toyota stakeholders"—The crux of a corporate culture challenge facing a Japanese company seeking to reconcile and balance a global perspective with traditional domestic values.

- "Communication in the Midst of Change"—Documenting the essential role of investor relations at AT&T; financial communications in an environment of strategic, market, and technological change.

- "Shadow Boxing," a two-way interaction between analysts and IR executives at BASF—A creative demonstration of the dual role of investor relations as an external corporate spokesperson and researcher/conduit of essential market information for senior management.

- "When less is more"—The essence of a simple but elegant and highly effective strategic and financial communications program at Schering-Plough.

- Finally (and from Chapter 2), "Simplicity, consistency and repetition"—The driving communications philosophy of GE Chairman and CEO Jack Welch; a communications approach that delivers the same message to outsiders (financial analysts and labor unions) and to insiders (the GE board and GE employees).[1]

KEY SUCCESS FACTORS

Strategic and Organizational Dimensions

Any discussion of the key success factors in strategic and financial communications must start at the top of the organization. The support, commitment, and active involvement of the chief executive officer is the sine qua non of an effective investor relations program. As the creator of strategic visions, a major shaper of corporate culture, and chief organizational spokesperson, the CEO is a prime contributor to a company's strategic credibility. Jack Welch at GE and Akio Morita at Sony are just two examples of the potentially dominant role that a company's chief executive officer can play in the conduct of corporate strategic and financial communications. On the other hand, a lack of CEO visibility and/or accessibility may have the opposite effect, dampening the enthusiasm of investors and analysts for a company and its prospects.

While the key to successful strategic and financial communications may start at the top of the organization, it certainly does not conclude at the peak of the corporate pyramid. Indeed, the hallmark of each of the successful investor communications programs reported in Part II was a closely knit, collaborative effort among senior management, investor relations officers, and corporate communications executives. The secret of an integrated, well-coordinated approach to strategic and financial communications may be partially attributed to the organization of IR activities, but a seamless communications effort appears to be more than the product of organization structure. In some of the companies discussed in Part II, IR reported to the chief financial officer; in other cases to corporate communications, and in other instances to the very highest levels in the organization. A common feature of all of the effective communications efforts was a close linkage among investor relations, corporate communications, and senior management. This critical bond was created and then cemented by the presence of a strong leadership figure representing the investor relations function. A strong leadership role, demonstrated by individuals who commanded great respect and credibility with their own senior management as well as within the investment community at large, runs as a common thread throughout most of the chapters in Part II. In the case of Toyota, where investor relations lacked a "dedicated" representative, a fragmentation of investor communications appears to have resulted in a lack of overall coordination in managing relationships with constituents in the investment community.

Another key success factor in the practice of investor relations is associated with the effective use of communications in turbulent and difficult environments. At AT&T and Toyota, changing markets, changing strategy, and/or changing technology challenged the financial communications capabilities of both companies. At AT&T, new technology was not only a source of turbulence, but also a tool used to inform the investment community of AT&T's strategic vision and the actions necessary to achieve a leadership position in new and emerging markets. Toyota, on the other hand, continues to struggle with the challenges imposed by an automobile industry in transition. As it searches for an effective strategy to cope with an industry facing severe economic and political pressures, Toyota appears to enjoy a comfortable cash position, a positive strategic reputation, and indications that it has employed its capital efficiently. In essence, Toyota enjoys a measure of strategic credibility that should allow it some "breathing room" to resolve the formidable problems it faces. Schering-Plough and Reuters offer further examples of companies operating in rapidly changing environments that have successfully employed technology and communications in the service of informing the investment community of their evolving strategic intentions—thereby enhancing their already considerable positive, strategic reputations.

Another hallmark of effective investor communications companies lies in their ability to respond successfully to the challenge of creating new corporate cultures that accommodate the realties of globalization and trends toward more open strategic and financial communications. At the General Electric Co. and at AT&T, communications have been a major driver of corporate culture change—at GE a process underway for well over a decade, while at AT&T a more recent activity. At Sony and Toyota, the delicate blending and balancing of globalization imperatives with more traditional Japanese domestic values generates a need for even more creative and candid communications initiatives. At BASF, top management support for an activist approach to investor communications contrasts sharply with a more conservative attitude toward strategic and financial disclosure typically found in many German corporations. Such a pioneering effort by BASF may offer some measure of encouragement to those Japanese companies that continue to search for a reconciliation between global capital-market realities and deeply embedded domestic values.

Key Success Factors and Emerging IR Role

World-class strategic and financial communications companies tend to anticipate rather than react to environmental pressures for change. Sony and BASF were leaders in their respective countries in recognizing the consequences and imperatives imposed by the globalization of capital markets. AT&T and Reuters were innovators in the development and use of advanced technologies, viewing these technologies as instruments—tools to leverage their progressive investor relations practices—rather than as ends in themselves. Schering-Plough was in the forefront of those companies that anticipated the evolution of the IR function from a passive financial communications activity to an active marketer of corporate equities to investors who are "customers" in every sense of the word. With the institutionalization of capital markets, progressive IR companies have been quick to respond to corporate governance issues, such as representation of outside directors on their boards. The institutionalization of markets has also encouraged leading IR companies to apply marketing-research techniques to identify diverse investor philosophies, goals, investment strategies, and specific information needs, and thus become more responsive to the needs of their customers.

In this evolving marketing role, investor relations executives become a link between the company and the investment community, informing and educating external constituencies about their companies' strategies, future direction, key products, and milestone events. In turn, these IR officers bring the views of external constituents, sharing these perspectives with senior management.

In order to function effectively in this expanded marketing role, investor relations officers in leading strategic and financial communications companies are becoming an integral part of management's "inner circle" and part of the "information loop." This places the IR executive at the core of the strategic nerve center of the company, which accomplishes two things: (1) It provides the IR manager with a strategic view of the organization and a source of strategic information that may be shared, as appropriate, with the investment community, and (2) it assures the necessary access to senior management in order to be able to inform and educate internal constituencies about the views of members of the investment community.

One way (but not the only way) to achieve a place in the inner circle is to enjoy a direct reporting relationship to the highest levels in the organization, as Sumio Sano did when he reported directly to Akio Morita, one of the founders of Sony. In other instances, proximity to the inner circle can be achieved by elevating the positional status of the IR function. As noted in Chapter 4, IR directors in Japan have been shifted from general manager levels to managing director levels in recent years. The same trends appear to be underway in the United States and Europe, at least among a number of more progressive IR companies. Further evidence of increased responsibility and stature likely to accrue to the IR function is beginning to surface as opportunities for an even more expanded IR role are emerging—a chance to become an active partner in the management of corporate assets and shareholder value.

In summary, the evolution of the IR function has proceeded further and faster in leading strategic and financial communications companies, moving from messengers of financial information to marketers of corporate equities to asset managers and collaborators in the process of shareholder value creation. The job of the IR officer in these companies has become more complex, interactive, strategic, significant, and responsible. IR executives increasingly occupy a place at the table within the inner circle of senior management, regularly participating in the strategic affairs and initiative of their companies. Strategic communications in world-class IR companies have become more candid, specific, timely, and future oriented, which has allowed them to reap the benefits and payoffs of more open disclosure while minimizing the costs and downside risks. This has contributed to a lower cost of capital, improved liquidity, and a larger and better-informed analyst following, which, in turn, has attracted an increased number of patient investors. In the long run, this can only lead to an improved share price and an enhancement of shareholder value.

Key Communications Characteristics

In addition to their innovative IR practices, leading strategic and financial communications companies do many of the same things that other companies do, the everyday, routine things, practicing the basic, time-tested principles of sound communications but doing so more effectively than other companies. For example,

- At Sony (as well as the other leading companies included in Part II), the company makes a determined effort to communicate during bad times as well as good. In 1984, when their Betamax-formatted VTR was about to lose out to the rival VHS format, Norio Ohga, former president of Sony, stood at the podium for thirteen hours during the 1984 shareholders meeting, answering all questions.
- At Schering-Plough, the guiding communications philosophy is to provide investors (and analysts) with exactly the information they need, when they need it, without frills—communications that have been described as "simple but elegant."
- At AT&T, during a period of turbulent change, "Communicating openly, fully and quickly is of utmost importance. It's what determines the level of confidence . . . constituents have in you. It's what determines your credibility" (Connie Weaver, AT&T, pp. 102–103).
- At Reuters PLC, "The keys to an effective investor relations program . . . are consistency in communications" (Michael J. Reilly). "We need to make sure that they [shareholders] understand us, what we do, how we do it, our

culture, aims, strategy and long-term ambitions so they can make a fair judgment about long-term prospects" (Geoffrey Wicks, p. 184).

- At BASF, "The strategic role of corporate communications and investor relations is clearly to prepare . . . ground for the financing requirements of tomorrow and thereafter" (Klaus D. Jessen, p. 160). "The best communication skills and efforts can only achieve their optimum effects in the context of a convincing 'strategic story' of the corporation. In an environment of disappointing operating performance, communications can support investors' long-term confidence and thereby limit downward pressure on share prices" (Klaus D. Jessen, pp. 157–158).

- At Toyota, harmonizing the interests of all stakeholders (customers, employees, and investors), rather than maximizing shareholder value, has had a significant impact on the nature and character of strategic and financial communications. Nevertheless, strategic communications at Toyota have been highly acclaimed and the company appears to enjoy a large measure of investor confidence and strategic credibility.

- Finally, the observations of GE Chief Executive Officer and Chairman John F. Welch: "If you have a simple, consistent message . . . you keep on repeating it . . . that's how you get through. It's a steady continuum that finally reaches a critical mass. . . . You communicate, you communicate and then you communicate some more. Consistency, simplicity and repetition is what it's all about."[2]

A Final Word About Communications: Past, Present, and Future

Candid communications about past performance, unadorned by self-serving attributions, is one very important feature of effective strategic and financial communications. Many U.S. and European companies could learn from Japanese corporations on this score. As our 1993 and 1998 global-strategy communications surveys revealed, Japanese companies are reluctant to take too much credit for good performance, while declining to attribute poor performance to external factors beyond management's control.

Openness, specificity, and timelines of communications are also highly valued characteristics and appear to be closely related to a company's strategic credibility within the investment community. While leading strategic and financial communications companies have been quick to recognize the importance of these communication characteristics, two recent surveys, discussed in Part I, provide a "good news–bad news" report on a larger population of companies. The good news comes from our 1998 global strategy communications update: The globalization and institutionalization of capital markets appear to be responsible for trends toward an increase in openness, specificity, and timeliness in financial communications in the United States,

Europe, and Japan. The bad news, which serves as a reality check and a measure of what still needs to be done, comes from our 1998 technology utilization survey: U.S. companies, at least, still have a ways to go in providing quality, specific, and timely strategic and financial information on the Internet, the crown jewel and brightest, most promising new communications technology development.

Communication about the future is another critical dimension of effective strategic and financial communications. Earlier research reported in Part I confirms this, while our 1998 global strategy communications update merely reaffirms this conclusion. Unfortunately, our 1998 survey also revealed a reduced willingness among U.S. companies to disclose strategic and financial information dealing with the future, at least relative to 1993 results and in comparison with a sample of European and Japanese companies.

Finally, and what probably has become a rallying cry for analysts and others in the investment community, "Communications during bad times as well as good" is the hallmark of effective strategic and financial communications. Regardless of the technology employed or the medium utilized to convey the message, consistent, candid, timely, specific, and open communications during difficult times as well as good has become the sine qua non of progressive and enlightened strategic and financial communications. As simple as this message is, many companies with conservative corporate communications cultures continue to resist the concept, long since embraced by leading strategic and financial communications companies.

NOTES

1. Robert Slater, *Jack Welch and the GE Way* (McGraw-Hill, 1999), 54.
2. Ibid., 54–55.

Selected Bibliography

Abegglen, J., and G. Stalk. *Kaisha: The Japanese Corporation*. New York: Basic Books, 1985.

AICPA Special Committee on Financial Reporting. Report prepared in 1991 at the request of the board of directors of AICPA.

"Annual Report Credibility." *Public Relations Journal* (November 1984): 31.

Arnold, J. "Communications and Strategy: The CEO Gets (and Gives) the Message." *Public Relations Quarterly* 33 (Summer 1988): 5–13.

Association for Investment Management and Research (AIMR). *Financial Reporting in the 1990's and Beyond*, prepared by Peter Knutson. 1992.

Bannister, Brendan D., and Richard B. Higgins. "Strategic Capability, Corporate Communications and Strategic Credibility." *Journal of Managerial Issues* 5 (Spring 1993): 92–108 (This article was based on a paper of the same title selected by the Business Policy and Planning Division of the Academy of Management for the Best Papers Proceedings at the 1991 annual meeting held in Miami, Florida.)

Bartlett, Christopher A., and Sumantra Ghoshal. *Managing Across Borders*. Boston: Harvard Business School Press, 1989.

Capital Choices. A research report presented to the Council on Competitiveness and cosponsored by the Harvard Business School, Executive Summary by Michael E. Porter.

Cossette, J. "Making Waves." *Investor Relations*, October 1997, 27–36.

"The Credibility Gap Widens." *Forbes*, 26 January 1987, 110.

"Credibility Is Critical." *Fortune*, 22 December 1986, 34.

Cusumano, M. *The Japanese Automobile Industry: Technology and Management at Nissan and Toyota*. Cambridge: Harvard University Press, 1985.

Dhaliwal, D. S. "Disclosure Regulations and the Cost of Capital." *Southern Economic Journal* 45 (1979): 785–794.

Diamond, D. W., and R. E. Verrechia. "Disclosure, Liquidity and the Cost of Capital." *Journal of Finance* 66 (1991): 1325–1359.

Diffenbach, John. "The Story That Should Be Told." *Public Utilities Fortnightly,* 25 May 1989.

Diffenbach, John, and Richard B. Higgins. "Strategic Credibility Can Make a Difference." *Business Horizons* 30 (May–June 1987): 13–18.

Dobson, J. "Corporate Reputation: A Free Market Solution to Unethical Behavior." *Business and Society* 28 (Spring 1989): 1–5.

Dorfman, Dan. "The Bottom Line: The Worst Annual Reports." *New York,* 10 June 1985, 17.

Dowling, G. "Managing Your Corporate Images." *Industrial Marketing Management* 15 (1986): 109–115.

Eccles, Robert G., and Sarah C. Mavrinac. "Improving the Corporate Disclosure Process." *Sloan Management Review* 36 (Summer 1995): 11–29.

Elliot, R. K., and P. D. Jacobson. "Costs and Benefits of Business Information Disclosure." *Accounting Horizons* 8, no. 4 (1994): 80–96.

Fombrum, Charles, and Mark Shanley. "What's in a Name? Reputation Building and Corporate Strategy." *Academy of Management Journal* 33 (1990): 233–258.

Foster, Geraldine U. "IR Today: The Changing Environment of Investor Relations." *Investor Relations Quarterly,* Summer 1997, 4–19.

Frederickson, J. W., and T. R. Mitchell. "Strategic Decision Processes: Comprehensiveness and Performance in an Industry with an Unstable Environment." *Academy of Management Journal* 27 (1984): 399–423.

Fruin, W. M. *The Japanese Enterprise System: Competitive Strategy and Cooperative Structures.* Oxford: Clarendon Press, 1992.

Hambrick, D., and A. Cannella. "Strategy Implementation as Substance and Selling." *Academy of Management Executive* 3 (1989): 278–285.

Higgins, Richard B. *The Search for Corporate Strategic Credibility: Concepts and Cases in Global Strategy Communications.* Westport, Conn.: Quorum Books, 1996.

Higgins, Richard B., and Brendan D. Bannister. "How Corporate Communication of Strategy Affects Share Price." *Long Range Planning* 25 (June 1992): 27–35.

———. "Corporate Communications: 'Frontrunners' vs. 'Challengers.'" In *1989/1990 Handbook of Business Strategy,* edited by Harold E. Glass. Boston: Warren, Gorham and Lamont, 1990.

Higgins, Richard B., and John Diffenbach. "Communicating Corporate Strategy—The Payoffs and the Risks." *Long Range Planning* 22 (June 1989): 133–139.

———. "The Impact of Strategic Planning on Stock Prices." *Journal of Business Strategy* 6 (Fall 1985): 64–69.

———. "Strategic Credibility—The Basis of a Strong Share Price." *Long Range Planning* 22 (June 1989): 10–18.

Japan Investor Relations Association. "Investor Relations Activities in Japan." *Tokyo Stock Exchange Magazine,* July 1998, 2–5.

Kajiwara, K., and T. Takagi. *Hikaku Nihon no Kaisha: Jidousha* (Comparison of Japanese companies: automobile). Tokyo: Jitsumu Kyoiku Shuppan, 1996.

Kohut, G., and A. Segars. "The President's Letter to Shareholders: An Examination of Corporate Communication Strategy." *Journal of Business Communication* 29 (Winter 1992): 7–21.

Lambert, R. "NY Exchange Sees Wider Horizons." *Financial Times*, 24 September 1997, 4.

Leontiades, M., and A. Tezel. "Planning Perception and Planning Results." *Strategic Management Journal* 1 (1980): 65–76.

Lev, Baruch. "Information Disclosure Strategy." *California Management Review* 34 (Summer 1992): 9–29.

Lundholm, Russell J. "How IR Influences Analysts: The Benefits of Better Disclosure." *Investor Relations Quarterly* 1 (Summer 1997): 46–50.

Marken, G. "Corporate Image—We all Have One, But Few Work to Protect and Project It." *Public Relations Quarterly* 35 (Spring 1990): 21–33.

"Net Worth." *Reputation Management* 13 (November/December 1997): 26–28.

Odaka, K., K. Ono, and F. Adachi. *The Automobile Industry in Japan: A Study of Ancillary Development.* Tokyo: Kinokuniya, 1988.

Petersen, Barbara K., and Hugh J. Martin. "CEO Perceptions of the IR Function: An Exploratory Study." *Investor Relations Quarterly* 1 (Summer 1997): 40–45.

Pincus, Theodore. "Full(er) Disclosure." *Reputation Management* 3 (May/June 1997): 30–32.

Reidenbach, R., and R. Pitts. "Not All CEO's Are Created Equal as Advertising Spokespersons: Evaluating the Effective CEO Spokesperson." *Journal of Advertising* 15 (1984): 30–36.

Rhyne, Lawrence C. "The Relationship of Strategic Planning to Financial Performance." *Strategic Management Journal* 7 (1986): 423–436.

Schaefer, Mary B. "Chief Executive: Chief Communicator." *MIT Management* (Spring 1993).

Slater, Robert. *Jack Welch and the GE Way.* McGraw-Hill, 1999.

Smith, P. "How to Present Your Firm to the World." *Journal of Business Strategy* 11 (January/February 1990): 32–36.

Sobol, Marion G., Gail E. Farrelly, and Jessica S. Taper. *Shaping the Corporate Image.* Westport, Conn.: Quorum Books, 1992.

Staw, Barry, Pamela I. McKechnie, and Sheila M. Puffer. "The Justification of Organizational Performance." *Administrative Science Quarterly* 28 (1983): 582–600.

"Taking Corporate Strategy Seriously." *Public Relations Journal* (August 1991): 32.

Togo, Y., and W. Wartman. *Against All Odds: The Story of Toyota Motor Corporation and the Family That Created It.* New York: St. Martin's Press, 1993.

Unseem, Michael. "Corporate Leadership in a Globalizing Equity Market." *Academy of Management Executive* 12 (November 1998): 43–59.

Uttal, B., A. Kantrow, L. Linden, and S. Stock. "Building R&D Leadership and Credibility." *Research Technology Management* 35 (May/June 1992): 15–24.

"Wall Street's Credibility Gap." *Business Week*, 23 November 1987, 92.

Welch, J. B. "Strategic Planning Could Improve Your Share Price." *Long Range Planning* 17 (February 1984): 144–147.

Yoshikawa, Toru. *Determinants of Investor Relations Strategy.* Ph.D. diss., York University, Toronto, Canada, 1997.

Index

Frederickson, J. W., 13

General Electric Company (GE):
corporate reporting practices of,
16; inaccurate perceptions of, 9–
10; level of strategic credibility of,
16
Global strategic and financial
communications, key success
factors: anticipate change, 165–
166; collaborative effort, 164;
communications—past, present,
and future, 168–169; creating new
corporate cultures, 165; effective
use of communications in difficult
environments, 165; everyday
things, 167–168; evolution of the
IR function, 167; involvement of
the CEO, 164; IR executives in the
inner circle, 166–167; random
impressions of, 163–164; strong
leadership, 164
Global strategy communications:
Japanese companies listed on the
NYSE, 44, 45; leading corporations
in the United States, Europe, and
Japan, 43–44, 45
Globalization of capital markets, 33–
34

Hogg, Christopher, 118

Idei, Nobuyuki, 127, 136, 137, 138,
139
Investor relations (IR): benefits of,
28–30; consequences of the
institutionalization of the U. S.
markets for, 24–25; corporate
glasnost, 28; expanded role of, 26–
27, 28; international efforts of, 25;
introduction to a discussion of,
23–24; technology impact on, 25;
world-class strategic communications companies in the forefront
of, 30. *See also under* Global
strategic and financial communications; *names of specific companies*
Investor Relations Quarterly, 2
Ishida, Taizo, 147

Isomura, Iwao, 149

Jacobson, P. D., 29
Japan Investor Relations Associa-
tion, 40. 42
Job, Peter, 110

Kogan, Richard Jay, 72, 74, 75

Lang, Mark, 28
Leontiades, M., 13
Lev, Baruch, 29
Luciano, Robert P., 74, 75, 78
Lundholm, Russell J., 28

Martin, Hugh J., 29
Mavrinac, Sarah C., 30
Mitchell, T. R., 13
Morita, Akio, 127, 130
Motorola. *See* Strategic credibility,
CEO credibility

National Investor Relations Institute, 3

Ohga, Norio, 125, 131
Okuda, Hiroshi, 154, 155, 157

Petersen, Barbara K., 29
Pincus, Theodore, 28
Plaugh, Abe, 73

Reuter, Paul Julius, 107
Reuters PLC: company's independence, 108–109; corporate structure, 110; history of, 111–112;
information and news products,
107–108, 114–116; Internet, 115,
120; media products, 116–117;
objectives, 112–113; television, 108,
116; transaction products, 116;
Trust Principles, 109; share history,
117–118
Reuters PLC IR program: Annual
Report, 120–121; audit and
surveys, 119; awards, 119–120;
day-to-day activities, 123; *Company Reporting* noted, 122–123;
integral part of overall operation,
118; Infoworld, 121; major inves-

About the Author and Contributors

Richard B. Higgins is the founder and managing director of Stratcom Associates of Grantham, New Hampshire, a management consulting firm specializing in strategic and financial communications. He is former professor of management at the College of Business Administration, Northeastern University, and visiting professor, International Management Development Institute, Lausanne, Switzerland. Dr. Higgins has consulted and lectured widely in the United States and Europe on the subjects of global strategy, strategic and financial communications, and strategic credibility. His articles have appeared in leading business journals. He began his career as an industrial engineer with E. I. DuPont de Nemours and Company before pursuing a career in academia and consulting. Dr. Higgins received his Ph.D. from the Graduate School of Business, Columbia University. This is his second book with Greenwood Publishing. His first work, *The Search for Corporate Strategic Credibility: Concepts and Cases in Global Strategy Communications*, was published by Quorum Books in 1996.

Mark W. Begor was appointed executive vice president and chief financial officer of NBC in April 1998. Begor is responsible for overseeing NBC's financial planning and operations, as well as playing a role in the company's strategic business initiatives. In August 1998 he assumed responsibility for NBC's global Management Information Systems Operations. Before coming to NBC, Begor spent eighteen years with General Electric. He was appointed a GE company officer in December 1996 after spending two years as GE's manager of investor communications. While in the investor communications role, Begor reported to the CEO and CFO of GE and was a member of GE's corporate executive council. Named investor relations officer of the year in 1997 and 1998 by *Investor Relations* magazine, Begor successfully led the company's communications with GE institutional and individual investors and Wall Street. Begor began his career with GE in 1980 in the financial management program. He joined GE's corporate audit staff in 1983, rising to the post of executive audit manager in 1987. Begor moved to GE Plastics in 1989 to become manager of operations analysis and financial support and was appointed director of finance and business development for GE Plastics Pacific, based in Singapore, in 1990. In 1993 he was named general manager of GE Plastics' Global Sourcing and Petrochemicals operation, where he led the revitalization of the global plastics sourcing process until being named to the investor communications position in 1995. Begor is a graduate of Syracuse University and holds an M.B.A. from Rensselaer Polytechnic Institute.

Geraldine U. Foster is senior vice president, investor relations and corporate communications, for Schering-Plough Corporation, a research-based company engaged in the discovery, development, manufacturing and marketing of pharmaceutical and health-care products worldwide. Ms. Foster joined the company in 1988 as vice president, investor relations, and was elected to her present position in 1994. Before coming to Schering-Plough, Ms. Foster was senior vice president, consumer credit, for the Connecticut Bank and Trust Company, where she also served as senior vice president, strategic planning. From 1984 to 1987 she was with the Continental Corporation in New York City, the parent company of Continental Insurance, holding the position of senior vice president, investor and corporate communications. From 1968 to 1984 she was affiliated with CBT Corporation in Hartford, Connecticut. Ms. Foster began her career at CBT Corporation in the investment research department and held various investment, banking and management positions. She holds a B.S. degree in Business Administration from Russell Sage College. Ms. Foster is a past chairman of the International Investor Relations Federation board of directors, a member of the executive committee of the Global Council of Investor Relations Executives, vice chairman of the board of Connecticut Innovations, Inc., vice chairman of the Eli Whitney Investment Advisory Committee, a member of the Knight-Bagehot Fellowship board of advisors at the Columbia University Graduate School of Journalism, and a member of the board of High Hopes Therapeutic Riding, Inc. She also is a member of the New York Stock Exchange Committee on Shareholder Communications, the Financial Accounting Standards Advisory Council, the Hartford Society of Financial Analysts, the Association for Investment Management and Research, the National Investor Relations Institute (where she previously served as a director), and the Investor Relations Association (where she previously served as president).

Stephen K. Galpin, Jr. is staff vice president, corporate communications, for Schering-Plough Corporation. Galpin is responsible for various aspects of the company's public-relations activities, including external publications, corporate media relations, employee communications, and providing communications support to the company's marketing and investor relations functions. He joined Schering-Plough in 1987 as manager, public information, and in 1992 was appointed director, public information. He was named director, corporate communications, in 1995. He previously was with Union Carbide Corporation as assistant manager, investor communications, in the corporate communications department. Prior to that he worked as a reporter for various Connecticut newspapers. Galpin earned a B.A. degree in English from Lake Forest College, Lake Forest, Illinois.

Peter Gregson is corporate publications manager for Reuters PLC. He joined Reuters as a graduate trainee journalist in 1966 after graduating from Leeds University, England, with a B.A. in English. During a thirty-year career as a foreign correspondent, Gregson was posted to Singapore, Hong Kong, China, Nigeria, South Africa, New York, Washington, and Zimbabwe. He has also held assignments in Iraq and the former Yugoslavia, was both a State Department and White House correspondent in Washington, and was Reuters's U.K. chief political correspondent and chief correspondent for the United Kingdom and Ireland. He took up his present position in 1996, assuming responsibility for producing Reuters's Annual Report and several internal communications functions.

Klaus D. Jessen is head of investor relations at BASF. Mr. Jessen finished his studies of business administration at the University of Hamburg with the Master Degree "Diplom Kaufmann." He worked for Dresdner Bank in different capacities from 1967 until 1973. In 1974 he joined the BASF Group, where he assumed responsibilities as a financial director of different group subsidiaries in Latin America. He was promoted to his current position in July 1987.

Yoshiko Sato is program director and senior research fellow at the Japan Investor Relations Association. Ms. Sato joined JIRA in May 1993. From 1985 until joining JIRA she worked for *Nihon Keizai Shimbun* (Japan Economic Journal), Japan's equivalent of the *Wall Street Journal*. In 1992 she was appointed as a principal staff member on the JIRA Establishment Committee and was later named program director upon JIRA's formal establishment. In this role, she has been planning and organizing most of JIRA's activities as well as editing and writing JIRA's journal. As senior research fellow, she has been in charge of two study groups at JIRA and has introduced various reports on IR matters. She earned her B.A. degree in Economics from Keio University and, in 1997, published a joint work on IR in Japan with Mr. Kazuhito Kondo. Ms. Sato is an alternate member of the governing council of IIRF.

Connie Weaver is vice president, investor relations and communications, for AT&T. Since 1996 she has led the telecommunications giant's financial, investor, and finance-employee communications efforts. This tenure has included her successful navigation of several key challenges, including megamergers, joint ventures, divestitures, new landmark federal telecommunications legislation, and AT&T leadership changes. Before joining AT&T, Weaver was senior director, investor relations, for Microsoft Corporation. She joined Microsoft in 1995 after five years as vice president, investor relations, for MCI Communications, and ten years in a variety of senior management positions at McGraw-Hill Corporation. She is a graduate of the University of Maryland.

Geoffrey Wicks is director, corporate relations, at Reuters PLC. He joined Reuters in 1978 as a sales executive with responsibility for brokers in London. In 1979 he became market manager for securities products. In 1981 he transferred to Paris to be marketing manager for the Western region, before moving to Stockholm eighteen months later as sales and marketing manager of the Nordic countries. He returned to London in 1987 as U.K. sales manager and became Northern region marketing manager, responsible for marketing in the United Kingdom, Nordic countries, and South Africa, eighteen months later. From 1991 to 1997 he held a number of senior business positions for the United Kingdom and Ireland. He took up his current position in May 1997 and is responsible at the group level for investor and media relations as well as corporate communications.

Toru Yoshikawa is a lecturer at the College of Commerce, Nihon University, in Tokyo. He received his Ph.D. from York University and M.A. from the University of Toronto. He has published papers on Japanese corporate governance in various academic journals, including *Advances in Comparative International Management, Business and the Contemporary World, Asia Pacific Business Review*, and *Nihon University Journal of Business*.